Praise for

"This outstanding book is critically needed in every home. Our current culture makes parenting, especially mothering, one of the most difficult tasks in history—Karol Ladd has pinpointed the main causes. She clearly explains how a loving mother can not only cope today but also thrive as one who is able meet the needs of her children and spouse. I am personally grateful for this greatly needed help for all our wonderful mothers."

—ROSS CAMPBELL, MD
Author, *How to Really Love Your Child* and *How to Really Parent Your Child*; and Clinical Associate Professor of Pediatrics and Psychiatry, College of Medicine, University of Tennessee

"Moms of all ages will be encouraged, refreshed, and filled with hope by Karol Ladd's practical and inspiring book, *Defuse*. They'll discover how to be filled with more love as they are drawn closer to Christ's heart for them and their children. A must-read for mothers!"

—CHERI FULLER
International Speaker and Best-selling Author,
A Busy Woman's Guide to Prayer and *The Mom You're Meant to Be*

"Karol Ladd's passion to equip moms to effectively minister to their children is evident on each page of this book. Her self-assessments and perceptive questions reveal to readers where they are in the positive parenting process. But most importantly, Karol skillfully presents solutions and suggestions that any mom can apply and begin today to become the mom God intends her to be. I heartily recommend it!"

—EDWINA PATTERSON
Founder, Redeeming the Time

"Karol Ladd helps us look at a painful reality known to all moms and gives us hope and direction without judging us and making us feel worse about ourselves. Thank you, Karol, for helping us face the difficult side of mother-hood with authenticity and boldness while showing us that it is never too late to be the moms we want to be. This book will give you the courage to face the destructive powers of a mom's anger then lead you to the greater power of God's grace."

—DR. DEBORAH NEWMAN
Licensed Marriage and Family Therapist;
Minister to Women, Christ Church, Plano, Texas; and
Author, *How to Really Love God as Your Father* and *Passion on Purpose*

Defuse

Books by Karol Ladd

A Positive Plan for Creating More Fun, Less Whining
A Positive Plan for Creating More Calm, Less Stress
The Power of a Positive Mom
The Power of a Positive Woman
The Power of a Positive Wife
The Power of a Positive Friend
The Power of a Positive Teen
The Power of a Positive Mom, Devotional & Journal
The Power of a Positive Woman, Devotional & Journal
The Frazzled Factor
Scream Savers
Table Talk
Fun House
Summer with a Smile
The Glad Scientist Series
Parties with a Purpose
Party Mix

Defuse

A Mom's Survival Guide to
More Love, Less Anger

KAROL LADD

THOMAS NELSON
Since 1798

NASHVILLE DALLAS MEXICO CITY RIO DE JANEIRO BEIJING

Published in Nashville, TN, by Thomas Nelson. Thomas Nelson is a trademark of Thomas Nelson, Inc.

Thomas Nelson, Inc. titles may be purchased in bulk for educational, business, fund-raising, or sales promotional use. For information, please e-mail SpecialMarkets@ThomasNelson.com

Library of Congress Cataloging-in-Publication Data

Ladd, Karol.
  Defuse : a mom's survival guide to more love, less anger / by Karol Ladd.
    p. cm.
  Includes bibliographical references and index.
  ISBN 13: 978-0-8499-0724-1 (trade paper)
  1. Anger. 2. Conflict management. 3. Mother and child. 4.
Mothers—Psychology. 5. Motherhood—Religious aspects—Christianity. 6.
Parenting—Religious aspects—Christianity. 7. Child abuse—Prevention.
I. Title.
  BF575.A5L3 2007
  152.4'70852—dc22   2006101147

Printed in the United States of America
07 08 09 10 11 RRD 9 8 7 6 5 4 3 2 1

Contents

Acknowledgments

A heartfelt thank-you to my friends at Thomas Nelson.

Debbie Wickwire, it is a great joy and privilege to work with you. Thank you for being a tremendous editor and an uplifting friend.

Jennifer Stair, you are a blessing to work with. You not only do a wonderful job of editing but also a great job of encouraging.

Most importantly, thank you to my precious family, Curt, Grace, and Joy, who encourage me, inspire me, and bless me. You are treasures!

Being the Mom You Meant to Be

Return to your rest, O my soul,
For the LORD has dealt bountifully with you.
—PSALM 116:7 NKJV

In all things it is better to hope than to despair.
—JOHANN WOLFGANG VON GOETHE

I used to be a fairly calm person until I had kids. Somewhere between "It's a girl!" and potty training two toddlers, my cool and collected spirit evaporated into thin air. I hate to admit it, but at times I became the motherhood version of Godzilla. Yes, Momzilla was alive! Oh don't get me wrong, I sincerely love my kids; but somehow motherhood was rattling me. What happened? Where did this latent anger come from, and why was it spewing out of my mouth like a volcano? This was not the mom I meant to be.

Perhaps it was the toys scattered everywhere or the never-ending laundry or changing three hundred diapers a day. Maybe it was the fact that I was functioning on fewer than four hours of sleep, while trying to keep everyone fed, clothed, and reasonably happy. I'm sure part of my tension had something to do with the reality that I could no longer come and go as I pleased. Even going to the grocery store to pick up a few items became a major ordeal.

Being a mom is a fast-track classroom to selflessness. In the

Motherhood School of Hard Knocks, we are continually stretched and pulled beyond our comfort zones. This tension tends to cause a fair amount of agitation and irritability. Mix in female hormones, toddler tantrums, and other daily life challenges, and the monster in all of us can emerge.

Dream Mom

When you were a little girl, how did you imagine yourself as a mom? What kind of picture did you have in your mind's eye of how you would run your home and care for your family? I'm guessing you probably didn't picture yourself yelling at your kids or feeling so frustrated you thought you would explode. The kind, gentle, and relaxed "dream mom" we all hoped to be didn't play out exactly that way in reality. We dreamed of a home filled with love, but what we got was a home filled with real people and an overload of responsibilities.

In the Motherhood School of Hard Knocks, we are continually stretched and pulled beyond our comfort zones.

Can our dreams still come true? Let me rephrase the question in more realistic terms. Can we create homes with more love and less anger? Yes! That's what this book is all about. I want to offer you solutions to strengthen the bonds of love in your home and dissolve much of the anger. I recognize that not all the anger in a home comes from the mom, so through the steps in this book, I want to help you not only deal with your anger but also respond wisely to anger that may erupt from your family members. Most importantly, our goal is to create in our homes an environment of love—a sincere love for each other and a deeper love for God.

Here's the Plan

You will notice that this book is divided into three sections, which are actually three steps to move you toward defusing the anger and increasing the love in your home. Our first survival step leads us to deal with our own anger as moms. After we identify the roots of anger lurking within, we will examine ways to reduce angry outbursts, disarm underlying bitterness, and guard our mouths from saying things that we ought not to say. All along we will ask God to gently teach us.

After we have dealt with our own anger, in the second survival step we will examine the stages of a child's development, because each stage presents a new set of issues and challenges (as well as joys). Often it is easy for us as moms to react instead of respond to our children's anger,

Our goal is to create in our homes an environment of love—a sincere love for each other and a deeper love for God.

so we'll learn wise responses for each stage of a child's life. Since we are talking about the entire family, I've included a chapter about how to handle your spouse's anger too. Whether you are married or separated from your husband, your response to him can make a world of difference in diffusing his anger.

The final survival step in our book leads us to building a loving environment. As much as we would like to think a loving environment just happens because we are a family, the reality is we need to encourage loving attitudes, actions, and words. If left unattended, the weeds of bitterness, jealousy, and unforgiveness can dominate the atmosphere of a family. As moms, we can encourage kindness, love, and respect between family members. Most importantly, we can inspire and cultivate a greater love of God.

True Love

My desire is to encourage you to build your home with love and encouragement. Honestly, I can't write a book about love unless I'm pointing to Christ and His great love for us. The Bible tells us that love comes from God. His love is abundant, sincere, and satisfying. I hope you will be refreshed by His care and love for you as you read this book.

If you have ever struggled with acknowledging God's great love toward you, then allow the words in this book to help you get rid of the doubt. At the end of each chapter, I've added a sweet encouragement to you in the form of *Love Notes from God*. Each love note includes a passage of Scripture highlighting a truth about God's love for us. When you are feeling down or unloved, I want you to go straight to these love notes from God and be strengthened and reassured of the fact you are sincerely loved by Him.

God's gracious love pouring through us can accomplish great things. It can overcome past hurts, it can help us forgive others, and it can give us hope when it seems there is no hope. I don't know exactly what your current family situation is, but I do know that there is a redeeming God who can heal your hurts whether big or small.

So join with me hand in hand, page by page, as we journey to a place of refreshment—a place where we, through God's strength, will help our family begin to experience more love and less anger.

Recognize and Deal With Your Anger

Create in me a clean heart, O God.

Renew a right spirit within me.

—Psalm 51:10 NLT

Our feelings, including the feeling of anger,

are God-given gifts that will serve us well if

we are able to be aware of them and act on them appropriately.

—Dwight L. Carlson, M.D.

Our first step toward building more love in our homes begins with God gently working on us. As we examine our heart issues and deal with any underlying anger, we take the first step toward increasing the love and decreasing the anger in our homes.

Anger Self-Assessment for Moms

I have fond childhood memories of running around with the neighborhood kids playing tag and hide-and-seek. (Yes, this was back in the days when it was safe to play around the neighborhood unsupervised.) One particular game of hide-and-seek is forever etched in my memory. It was the time I found a perfect hiding place deep within the branches of a giant evergreen bush. I remember wondering, *Why hasn't anyone ever hidden here before?* The answer became painfully clear to me within a few seconds. Wasps had made their home in this most perfect of hiding places!

As you can imagine, I never went back to that hiding spot again. I couldn't believe those wasps got so mad at me. What did I do to them? Well, I guess I did intrude on their territory and compromise the tranquil safety of their nests. When you look at it from the wasps' point of view, it's no wonder they get angry and sting people. The busy wasps work tediously for days to create a complex, multilevel wasp haven, then some careless kid comes along and disrupts their whole world. All that work completely dismantled by one little kid! What frustration!

Sometimes that's the type of frustration we feel as moms. We work hard all day and night to love and care for the needs of our families, and what do we get in return? A messed-up house, a disrupted schedule, and the exasperation of being pulled in every direction, mixed with lots of whining and very little appreciation. It's enough to make you want to sting someone! And unfortunately that's what we do sometimes. Our words, actions, and attitudes can hurt or sting the people around us—but unlike wasp stings, which heal and soon go away, a mother's stinging words can last a lifetime.

> Everyone experiences anger at times, but the important aspects are how we deal with it and how we choose to express it.

Now, let me reassure you that anger is a normal, God-given emotion. Everyone experiences anger at times, but the important aspects are how we deal with it and how we choose to express it. A pattern of angry explosions is not healthy in building love and communication in our homes, and our kids will likely pick up the pattern of anger in their own lives. I'm sure you don't want your kids to reflect on your anger when they think about you. Neither do I!

So how do we handle our anger wisely? We begin by recognizing what tends to trigger our own anger. We also need to explore any underlying issues that may stir up anger in our hearts and emotions.

In this chapter, you are going to walk through a personal assessment created just for you as a mom. The goal is to help you discover a little more about yourself and what is eating at you both internally and externally. Then in the following chapters, we will examine ways to deal with our anger and express it wisely.

The One Who Knows Our Hearts

If you are like me, you can't see your own heart very well. I can hardly see any of my own issues, but it sure seems easy to see everyone else's. Honestly, it's difficult to step back and take an accurate view of ourselves. We need God's insight to examine and tend to our heart issues. As we begin our soul-searching anger self-assessment, let's start by seeking God's wisdom and direction. He is able to reveal what we cannot see about ourselves. With God's assistance, we can begin to discover the changes we need to make. God is our loving designer and creator. He knows us better than we know ourselves.

King David recognized his need for God's help when it came to understanding himself. In Psalm 139, David acknowledged:

O LORD, You have searched me and known me.
You know my sitting down and my rising up;
You understand my thought afar off.
You comprehend my path and my lying down,
And are acquainted with all my ways.
For there is not a word on my tongue,
But behold, O LORD, You know it altogether.
You have hedged me behind and before,
And laid Your hand upon me.
Such knowledge is too wonderful for me;
It is high, I cannot attain it.
Search me, O God, and know my heart;
Try me, and know my anxieties;

And see if there is any wicked way in me,
And lead me in the way everlasting. (vv. 1–6, 23–24 NKJV)

When we think about the fact that God knows all about us, it can be overwhelming and frightening at the same time. He knows our thoughts (yikes!), our actions (eek!), and our intent (oh my!), yet He loves us anyway. What an amazing love! His love overflows with mercy and grace! Let us humbly come to Him and ask Him to give us eyes to examine ourselves.

Pray with me:

Gentle and loving heavenly Father, You deserve all praise and glory, for You know all things and can do all things. You know all about me. You know how I am wired, how I think, and how I react, yet You love me with an everlasting love. You are truly the Good Shepherd, tenderly caring for my life. Thank You that You are the God who sees all.

Lord, I know You see my heart and the issues of anger in my life. I confess I cannot see my own issues. I need Your help. Help me to take an honest look at the role anger plays in my communication with my family. Ever so gently open my eyes so that I may see and turn from what is wrong. In Your loving way, lead me to a new place, a place of love and kindness. Allow me to reflect Your abundant, grace-filled love in my words and actions toward my family.

Thank You for healing my wounds and giving me the help I need. In Jesus' name, amen.

Anger Self-Assessment for Moms

This is your opportunity to be open, honest, and real. You don't need to show the following self-assessment to anyone. It's yours, and it's personal. (Warning: if you are going to let a friend borrow this book, you may want to tear out these pages or white-out your answers.) There is no final score on this self-assessment because our goal is to learn more about ourselves and un-cover how our anger affects us. Our goal is not to slap a label or a grade on our anger in order to see how much better or worse off we are than others. Sorry, you won't be able to go over to your friend's house and compare scores!

> In order to resolve anger-related challenges, we need to recognize how anger is manifested in our lives.

This assessment will examine four crucial areas. First, we will take a candid look at our-selves and identify our anger. Then, we will examine our current state of well-being and the factors that may be raising our levels of anger. Next, we will look at specific situations and circumstances—both internal and external—that may trigger our anger. Finally, we will look at how we express our anger.

In order to resolve anger-related challenges, we need to recog-nize how anger is manifested in our lives. Don't be afraid to be trans-parent here. Ready? Let's jump right in.

Section One: DESCRIPTION OF ANGER

Identify the paragraph that best fits where you are right now.

❏ You have times of slight anxiety or irritability, but few things rattle you. Agitation is short lived, and your kids can't even remember the last time you lost your temper. You discipline with firmness and love. You are able to discern what is worth getting angry about and what needs to be dropped. When you are angry, you handle it appropriately.

❑ You experience an increased level of irritation and anxiety when plans change or something goes wrong. You get agitated at unexpected messes or spills and speak sternly with the kids when you have "had enough." There are occasional days when you feel frazzled and short-tempered. When frustration or stress builds, you sometimes lose it with the kids, but you regret it, apologize, and vow never to do it again.

❑ You struggle most days not to lose your temper. Little things get to you, and you rarely seem to have joy. You accuse and lash out at those around you. You speak (or shout) before you think because of the anger welling up inside you. At times you worry that you may be dangerous with your words or punishment. You fear losing control. You have lost control more times than you would like to admit. The mistakes or mess-ups of others (usually the kids) feel like a personal affront.

❑ You feel helpless in your battle with stress and anger. You wake up each day just hoping you can make it through without hurting those you love. Yelling has become second nature. The way you express your anger is unhealthy and you know it, but you can't seem to do anything about it. Resentment, anger, and hatred seem to control your inner thoughts. You are a ticking time bomb, and anything can set you off.

At this point, let's go back through the descriptions and reflect for a moment. I realize that there is no perfect description that fits you exactly because you are a unique creation, but I do want you to highlight or underline any sentences or phrases that seem to match you exactly. Ask the Lord to reveal to you any areas of self-denial that need to be addressed. Allow this exercise to be a mirror for you to see some things you typically don't see about yourself—yet be gentle with yourself. Remember, anger is common to us all, and the point of this book is to help us come to a place of handling our anger wisely. If you identified with the fourth level, please find someone you can talk to immediately. Seek help and accountability.

Section Two: YOUR CURRENT STATUS

How would you describe yourself emotionally? Check the ones that describe you.

I am typically . . .

☐ Balanced, content, have a general feeling of well-being
☐ Worried, anxious, fretful
☐ Overwhelmed, frazzled, frustrated
☐ Discontent, needy, unsettled
☐ Bitter, angry, hostile
☐ Beating myself up with guilt and regrets
☐ Depressed

What is your current physical condition? Make a mark on each line at the place that seems to best describe where you are right now.

Tired all the time ←————————————————→ Well rested

Never take vitamins ←————————————————→ Take daily multiple vitamins

Eat junk most of the time ←————————————————→ Eat healthy foods

Overweight or underweight ←————————————————→ Healthy weight

←————————————————————————————→
    Never exercise   Consistently exercise

←————————————————————————————→
    Often sick   Generally healthy

Do you have a chronic illnesses or debilitating pain? _____
Does your current physical state seem to affect your ability to handle anger? _____

Socially speaking, how would you describe your relationships outside of your family?

Generally, I . . .
❑ Have several deep and meaningful friendships
❑ Keep to myself and don't interact with many people
❑ Have a large circle of friends and acquaintances
❑ Have trouble keeping friends
❑ Have difficulty making new friends
❑ Enjoy several good friendships but would like to have more meaningful ones

Are your friends a source of refreshment to you? _____
Do you have a friend with whom you can talk about your anger?

_____

How would you describe yourself spiritually? Check the ones that apply.

Currently, I . . .
❑ Have no spiritual input or growth
❑ Attend church, but nothing more

❑ Desire to grow deeper in my faith and knowledge of God

❑ Am actively growing in my relationship with Christ

❑ Passionately pursue Christ in all I say and do at church and
at home

Does your relationship with God give you strength in the daily cares
of life? _____

What is your financial situation? Check all that apply.

When it comes to my finances, I am . . .

❑ In serious financial debt

❑ Struggling to pay the bills each month

❑ Spending more than I earn

❑ Breaking even with income and outflow

❑ Financially stable

❑ Regularly saving and investing

❑ Tithing at least 10 percent of my income

❑ Financially well-off with no worries

Is your current financial situation a source of tension and stress?

_____

How would you describe your living environment? Mark a place on
each line that best describes your current situation.

Constantly noisy   Generally calm

Chaotic   Orderly

Dark   Bright

Does your living environment seem to be a source of agitation or anger? _____

How would you describe your relationships with your family? Mark a place on the line that describes the following relationships.

◄————————————————————————►

Spouse: Loving and encouraging   Hateful and disjointed

◄————————————————————————►

Kids: Healthy relationship   Strained relationship

◄————————————————————————►

In-laws: Very close   Distant or estranged

◄————————————————————————►

Your family of origin: Very close   Distant or estranged

Are any of the above relationships a source of stress and anger to you?_____

How would you describe the way your parents communicated with you and treated you as a child?

_____

_____

Do you have any resentment toward your parents and the way they treated you as a child?

_____

_____

Were you abused by your parents or other adult in any way?

_____

Are you harboring bitterness against anyone, or is there someone you need to forgive?

_____

Do you feel hatred toward anyone right now? _____

Do you feel overly pressured by someone to do things you are not able to do?

_____

Are you currently frustrated with a family member because he or she is not meeting your expectations?

_____

After completing Section Two, go back through your answers and highlight or circle any areas in your life that tend to be sources of bitterness, frustration, or anger. Ask the Lord to show you if there are any changes or improvements you can make. I'm not saying to place blame on your situation, but rather to see if you can identify any areas in which you can make positive changes.

If you are dealing with some forgiveness issues, begin asking the Lord to help you forgive and heal the hurts. We will walk through several steps toward victory in the area of forgiveness in Chapter 14. For right now, I want you to recognize the sources of your anger so you can work toward healthy solutions.

Section Three: ANGER TRIGGERS

Consider the following possible triggers that may set off your anger. Determine the level of intensity the trigger instills (1 being a trigger that most often tends to create your explosion and 10 being a trigger that just makes you a little hot under the collar). Cross out any that are not a factor at all in your life.

_____ Kids' whining or tantrums

_____ Childish behaviors (spilling juice, forgetting homework, etc.)

_____ Bickering among siblings

_____ Monthly hormones

_____ Messy or disorderly home

_____ Hurt or criticism from spouse

_____ Finances

_____ Irresponsibility of others (husband or kids)

_____ Too many people needing you at once

_____ Trying to get somewhere or being late

_____ Time of day, tired and hungry

_____ Other_____

_____ Other_____

Is there someone in particular who seems to set your anger on fire? _____

Are you angry with God about anything right now? _____

We will refer back to this information when we get to Chapter 5, dealing with the "mommy explosion."

Section Four: EXPRESSIONS OF ANGER

Anger and frustration can be manifested in different ways. Respond to each of the following descriptions thoughtfully and honestly.

When I'm angry, I . . .

	Always	*Sometimes*	*Rarely*	*Never*
Use the silent treatment				
Scream and yell				
Throw things				
Belittle others				
Use sarcasm				
Inflict physical pain on others				
Accuse and blame				
Work toward a calm discussion				
Stick to the facts at hand				
Choose to forgive				
Think clearly				
Seek practical solutions				
Secretly keep things bottled up inside				
Other:_____				

When you express your anger, do you feel a need to apologize? _____

Why or why not?

_____

What do you fear most about your anger? _____

What changes do you know you need to make in your personal
anger management?_____

_____

What have you learned about yourself by taking this assessment?

_____

Now What?

My hope is that by completing this self-assessment, you discovered important truths about yourself and identified some characteristics about your anger. Maybe some of it you wanted to see and maybe some you didn't. You probably already knew deep down inside several of these issues existed in your life, but perhaps you didn't want to recognize them.

If we are going to work toward handling our anger in a healthy way, we need to honestly examine ourselves. Don't be hard on yourself or wallow in regret. Instead, choose to move in a positive direction and grow from what you have learned. With God all things are possible. He is able to redeem our lives. Through the work of His Spirit, we are able to grow to be more like Jesus, but the first step is to recognize our neediness. God is continuing to do a great work within each of us. No one is a perfect finished product.

> If we are going to work toward handling our anger in a healthy way, we need to honestly examine ourselves.

As we begin to recognize key areas of our lives on which we want to work, our next step is to get a handle on how to manage and express our anger wisely. Let's recognize that we are all fellow strugglers in need of God's gentle Spirit. With His help and guidance, we can build our homes with encouragement and love instead of tearing them down with our bitterness and anger. Are you willing to move forward and be the mom you meant to be? Congratulations, you are moving in the right direction by being honest with yourself and looking forward to what God can do in the future.

Love Notes from God

The LORD has appeared of old to me, saying:
"Yes, I have loved you with an everlasting love;
Therefore with lovingkindness I have drawn you.
Again I will build you, and you shall be rebuilt." (Jer. 31:3–4 NKJV)

Oh the beauty of God's everlasting love and restoring power! No other love can compare to His. He knows us, He sees our hearts, yet He chooses to love us with a merciful, everlasting love. This love is not reserved for "perfect Christians" who do everything God wants them to do with no mistakes. No, the Lord knows we all fail. His love reaches down and touches the wretched, weak, and brokenhearted. He redeems our lives through Christ and rebuilds our relationships through the power of His Spirit working in us.

Look to Him, my friend. See His everlasting love and His arms open wide, calling you to Himself. Don't wallow in the past; instead, allow the Lord to rebuild your life with His kindness.

■ ■ ■

How does God's great love for me free me to be more honest about myself?

2

What's Worth Getting Angry Over and What's Not

The discretion of a man makes him slow to anger,
And his glory is to overlook a transgression.

—PROVERBS 19:11 NKJV

Anybody can become angry—that is easy;
But to be angry with the right person,
and to the right degree, and at the right time,
and for the right purpose, and in the right way—
that is not within everybody's power and is not easy.

—ARISTOTLE

The first time I left our two precious daughters alone with my husband, Curt, was a complete disaster. Why couldn't he simply follow the detailed instructions I had given him? Was it too hard to feed them the highly nutritious lunch I had carefully spelled out in my lengthy handwritten instructions? Was there some reason he couldn't look at the clock and put them down for their naps at the exact time I usually put them down?

And what happened to story time before their nap? Forget the fact that he didn't change one diaper. He completely ignored the schedule I had planned. It's a miracle our girls survived that horrific aberration of their normal routine while I was away for three hours!

Of course, I was convinced that it was my duty to make sure this never happened again. We don't need to go into all the ugly details at this point, but suffice it to say I let a little anger seep through as my husband and I "discussed" his babysitting skills. Now I can look back at the incident, laugh, and say, "I can't believe I got so worked up about things that don't really matter!" At the time, it seemed so important.

> The early rumblings of anger often show up without warning.

How do we know when to overlook a fault or annoyance? When do we allow things to bug us enough to make changes? And how do we know if we are simply repressing our anger? We will address all of these important questions in this chapter. Let's begin with a clarification. Often before we feel the emotion of anger, we feel a primary emotion. Frustrated, irritated, pressured, attacked, intimidated, worried, disrespected, offended, guilty, and frightened are all examples of feelings we may experience throughout a typical day. I call them the early rumblings of anger. If these feelings intensify and grow, they can lead to angry outbursts or bitterness or unforgiveness.

The early rumblings of anger often show up without warning. It is good and healthy to recognize and identify these primary feelings of anger. For instance, you are waiting in line at the grocery store (and of course you are in the slowest line), and one of your kids becomes irritable and starts whining. You may identify that you are feeling frustrated or impatient or even intimidated or embarrassed, and those emotions could potentially move into serious, full-blown anger.

Although we usually do not choose our initial feelings, we can choose what we will do with them. If we choose to focus on our hurts, frustrations, and irritations, they can fester and grow and become deep-seated anger or an ugly outward expression. We all tend to handle our anger in different ways. Some people repress their anger and stuff it deep down inside until it eventually explodes. Others express their anger in rage or other hurtful ways, while some people use their anger as a catalyst for change and express it in a healthy way. We'll talk more about healthy ways to express our anger in the next chapter.

> Let's admit it, on any given day we can take a small issue and make it into a big one if we choose.

The roots of anger typically are born out of a feeling of injustice. In the Bible, we read about God's anger in numerous cases. Certainly His anger is a true, righteous anger based on immorality or injustice. We see God's anger in the Old Testament directed toward idolatrous nations or disobedient Israelites, and we see it in the New Testament as Jesus exhibited anger toward the Pharisees and the money changers in the temple. Although our anger is also typically based on a perceived injustice or sense of being wronged, unfortunately, our anger is not so pure. Our anger is usually filtered through our own self-centeredness and sinful natures.

In this chapter, we will examine the possibility that some things are just not worth the anger. Yes, we all experience the early rumblings of anger throughout any typical day as moms, but there are some issues we don't need to dwell on or allow to grow into full-blown anger. Let's admit it, on any given day we can take a small issue and make it into a big one if we choose. As wise moms, we want to develop the discernment to see that some things just aren't worth getting upset over.

Now, I know it's downright hard sometimes to keep our feelings from boiling over into full-blown anger. How do we grow to that point of self-control? It begins with our focus.

Focus, Flexibility, and Forgiveness

Perspective is everything. Who among us doesn't get caught up in mommy minutia from time to time? You know, the little things we think are absolutely essential to making our children's world a perfect place, like having the perfect stroller, the nicest teacher, and, of course, only highly nutritious lunches each day. Amid our myriad responsibilities, we often end up getting frazzled over nonessential things.

When we step back and see the big picture, we realize our kids will survive even if their lunch isn't "perfect" every single day. If their schedule gets a little off for a few days at Grandma's, they are not ruined for life. Honestly let it go if your husband didn't get them in bed until a half hour after their normal bedtime. Focusing on the big picture and seeing things from a wider view will help us through tense moments. In the big scheme of life, many issues are simply worth dropping.

Perspective is also important when it comes to worrying about the future. Often we can get all worked up over what-ifs. We may feel extremely frustrated when our child in potty training has yet another accident, and we begin to worry. *What if she never gets out of diapers?* Or our child makes a B on a spelling test, and we become irritated. *What if he doesn't get into college?* Now these are silly extremes, but we can dissipate a large amount of anger if we choose not to let future what-ifs skew our perspective from the here and now.

Flexibility is another trait that will help us through life. As my neighbor says, "A flexible woman rarely gets bent out of shape." I love it! Frustration and anger often erupt when we get rigid in our ways and feel as though everything must go exactly according to our plans or schedules. It's all well and good to make a plan and try to keep things on schedule, but you and I both know the reality is very few things happen exactly as planned. Circumstances change often in ways that are out of our control. A child gets sick, traffic makes you late, or an unexpected phone call gets you off schedule. You can live your life angry at these constant interruptions to your plan, or you can make a conscious decision to be flexible and not let it get to you.

I know you can't snap your fingers and say, "I will not care about the little things anymore." But you can gradually train yourself, with God's help, to be able to say, "Oh well, this really doesn't matter in the big scheme of things." Flexibility is born out of the big-picture perspective, recognizing that change is inevitable and typically not worth getting worked up over.

The Big-Picture Viewpoint Toward Others

When we focus on the irritations or annoyances of another person, they usually become larger than life. Isn't it sad that we generally focus on the faults and shortcomings of those who are closest to us? We only hope they never focus on our weaknesses to such a degree! Our first step is to change our focus and get our minds off the irritant. Certainly there are times when we need to approach another person about a problem or annoyance, while other times we need to bear with the person, recognize that he or she may do things differently, and forgive the person if necessary.

Being patient with someone doesn't come naturally. It's actually much easier to yell at someone. Yet this is one of those times when the easier route is not the most prudent one. In fact, blowing up in anger at someone can have long-term negative consequences and rarely brings about the intended result or change. We may not be able to overlook someone's faults in our own strength and power, but God's love pouring through us can be life changing. As we struggle to bear with another individual, let us first take our eyes off of that person and his or her faults. Then we can turn our eyes upward toward the Lord's great love.

Proverbs 19:11 reminds us, "The discretion of a man makes him slow to anger, and his glory is to overlook a transgression" (NKJV). We become slaves to whatever masters us— and if we allow our emotions to control us, we become slaves to our anger. We have a choice about what we will allow to fester and grow. It begins with our minds. As we turn our focus onto the bigger picture and choose to overlook certain faults, we take the first steps to the mature decision to overlook an affront.

> We have a choice about what we will allow to fester and grow. It begins with our minds.

The Power of Waiting

There have been many times in my life when I've abruptly unleashed my anger, yet later looked back and thought, *Why did I get so angry about that? It just wasn't worth it.* Whether it is with our kids or with our spouses or with a neighbor, there is wisdom in waiting. When we feel those initial feelings of anger, it is wise for us to give ourselves a cooling-off period of time. Then we can revisit the issue, but hopefully our tempers have cooled and we are not experiencing that initial passion.

I could have dissuaded many an argument with my husband, Curt, if I had simply waited to cool off instead of approaching him in the heat of my emotions. Allowing an hour or two to pass gives our burning emotions an opportunity to cool off, allowing us to think a little more clearly. When we determine to allow some time to pass, we have the option to revisit the issue (so we are not ignoring it), but more importantly, we have time to determine if it really is an issue. We may recognize our hormones may be getting the better of us, or we may be able to step back out of our frustration and see the bigger picture.

James urges us to be slow to anger. "My dear brothers, take note of this: Everyone should be quick to listen, slow to speak and slow to become angry, for man's anger does not bring about the righteous life that God desires" (1:19–20). Fools rush in, but the wise wait. Give yourself an intentional interval of time to cool off, and then revisit the issue. If there is still a reason to proceed and make positive changes, then move forward gently and in control of your emotions.

Overlooking an Offense Versus Repressing Your Anger

Psychologists warn about suppressed or repressed anger, telling us not to ignore or stuff our anger or we will eventually explode. They're right. We must be careful not to ignore underlying bitterness or anger and allow it to fester inside us. On the other hand, there is a selfless wisdom in recognizing that a situation is frustrating, but we're not going to let it bother us. Perhaps our society has become a little "repressaphobic." *If I overlook this, then I may be repressing my anger,* we think.

What's the difference between repressing anger and overlooking an offense? Generally speaking, a woman represses anger when someone or something has deeply hurt or angered her, yet she chooses to ignore the pain or even deny it. She may not even recognize that she is stuffing her hurt or pain, but she has not let go of it. She is holding on to it deep inside. On the other hand, a woman who overlooks an offense acknowledges her feelings of frustration or irritation, yet she makes a conscious decision to forgive or let it go. She relinquishes the right to hold on to a grudge or coddle a bitter thought. She takes her eyes off the irritation and doesn't go back to it over and over again.

As you read this, you may realize you have trouble overlooking an offense. Please don't think this speaks badly of you. I'm thankful you are being honest. The truth is that we all have different personalities. Some of us are naturally more concerned about details, and some of us are extremely laid back. It is not necessarily a spiritual issue (although it can be), but it can be a personality trait as well. Don't go on a guilt trip if you struggle to let go of something that irritates you. Look at it as an opportunity to seek God's help and wisdom and ask for His discretion as you slowly let go of little stuff. Learning to overlook and let go of offenses is a challenging process, but we must remember it is a *process* that with time can become a new habit.

> Learning to overlook and let go of offenses is a challenging process, but we must remember it is a *process* that with time can become a new habit.

Let's distinguish a few traits or characteristics of overlooking an offense versus repressing anger:

Overlooking an Offense	Repressing Anger
Consciously forgiving an offense	Refusing to forgive an offense
Choosing not to focus on the pain	Rehearsing the hurt

Overlooking an Offense	*Repressing Anger*
Loving thoughts	Hateful or self-destructive thoughts
Gracious spirit	Judgmental spirit, irritability
Recognizing God's sovereignty	Filled with blame toward others
Sincerely letting things roll off of you	Taking things personally
Confronting in love	"Blowing up" or raging at people or avoiding needed confrontation

Ignoring our feelings or stuffing our anger can lead to a dangerous explosion of emotions, so we must be careful not to mistake overlooking an irritation with suppressing our feelings. Ultimately, there is a tight walk between stuffing our hurt and letting go of it. The bottom line is we must be true to ourselves. Truth says, "I want to let this go, but it is honestly still bothering me, so I'm going to need to deal with it." Being honest with ourselves is a painful process, but it brings us to the God of truth, who knows us better than we know ourselves. Let us humbly come before Him and ask Him to help us recognize any hidden anger.

> Being honest with ourselves is a painful process, but it brings us to the God of truth, who knows us better than we know ourselves.

Questions to Ask Ourselves

When we find ourselves experiencing the early rumblings of anger (such as frustration, irritation, fear, guilt, or intimidation), we can ask ourselves certain questions to help us discern if we need to simply let it drop, wait for a while, or intentionally deal with the issue. Don't go through the entire list of questions below every time you feel an angry emotion, but pick out a few questions that you know would help you personally. Highlight those particular questions you recognize will be helpful to you in your own hot spots of anger. These questions are intended to help you regain your focus and move toward self-control.

- Am I focusing on the big picture, or am I stuck on small stuff?
- Is this an opportunity to teach my child? If so, is screaming going to teach her?
- Has my child disobeyed, shown disrespect, or been dishonest? If so, how will I discipline him in order to help him learn to turn from the behavior?
- Are my expectations too high for a child of this age?
- Am I basing my anger on truth or assumptions?
- Am I acting out of love for the other person?
- What does God want to teach me through this situation or person?
- Am I responding from a root of pride?
- Is my motive in the best interest of the other person, or am I only thinking of my own interests?
- Is there something else that is really eating at me?
- Is it that time of the month?

- Am I being flexible?
- Am I trying to see the other person's viewpoint?

The Power to Choose

Flexibility, focus, and forgiveness are tools that can help us when we are faced with the frustrations life brings. They assist us in being slow to anger and overlooking an affront. When I told a friend of mine the title of this chapter, she shared her perspective. "What's worth getting angry over? After years of struggling with anger, I have finally realized that the answer to that question is *very little*. There are very few things in life worth getting angry over, and even that anger can be used in a positive way."

So I ask you: as a mom, what is worth getting angry over? Think about the bottom line of what is worth your anger. For me, it came down to if my kids were disobedient, disrespectful, or dishonest. Those were the three biggies worth getting angry over—though even in my anger it was important not to sin, but rather to teach and train my kids. My anger was not against them, but against their behavior. Oh, I'm not saying those are the only things I got angry over; I am saying I believe they were the only things worth getting angry over.

In the space below, list specific issues that seem important enough to ignite your anger. Notice I'm only leaving a small space as I hope you don't need too much.

_____

_____

_____

_____

_____

Although we cannot choose the emotions that first enter our hearts and minds, we can choose whether we allow them to fester and grow. There are some battles not worth fighting, while others need to be handled in a wise way.

It benefits us (and those around us) to learn to let some things go or else we will become irritable, angry women. And if you're like me, you don't want to be that kind of mom. Although motherhood is filled with loving and joyful moments, there are also times of challenges and frustrations. There are times we may be extremely irritated and can't seem to let it go, so we must choose to handle our anger appropriately and make necessary changes. I want you to know every mom reading this book knows the feeling of letting their emotions get the best of them at times. Every one of us needs God's help in dealing with our anger and in choosing what is worth the anger.

How wonderful that we can come before the Lord and seek His help! David wrote, "This poor man called, and the LORD heard him; he saved him out of all his troubles" (Ps. 34:6). We may be weak, but our God is strong. We may lack discernment, but our loving heavenly Father has all wisdom.

I'm sure you are familiar with the Serenity Prayer. This poem reminds us that we can call on Jesus and ask for His help and wisdom as we face each day's frustrations.

Serenity Prayer

God grant me the serenity
to accept the things I cannot change;
courage to change the things I can;
and the wisdom to know the difference.
Living one day at a time,

enjoying one moment at a time,
accepting hardship as the pathway to peace;
taking, as He did, this sinful world as it is,
not as I would have it;
trusting that He will make all things right
if I surrender to His will;
that I may be reasonably happy in this life,
and supremely happy with Him forever
in the next.
Amen.

Love Notes from God

Yet the LORD *longs to be gracious to you;*
> *he rises to show you compassion.*
For the LORD *is a God of justice.*
> *Blessed are all who wait for him!* (Isa. 30:18)

He tends his flock like a shepherd:
> *He gathers the lambs in his arms*
and carries them close to his heart;
> *he gently leads those that have young.*

He gives strength to the weary
> *and increases the power of the weak.*
Even youths grow tired and weary,
> *and young men stumble and fall;*
but those who hope in the LORD
> *will renew their strength.*
They will soar on wings like eagles;

they will run and not grow weary,
   they will walk and not be faint. (Isa. 40:11, 29–31)

So do not fear, for I am with you;
   do not be dismayed, for I am your God.
I will strengthen you and help you;
   I will uphold you with my righteous right hand. (Isa. 41:10)

These words from Isaiah offer us a blessed hope as moms. I feel so completely loved as I read the words of compassion and care God has for His people. Isaiah spoke these words to the Israelites—not to "perfectly following the Lord" Israelites but to the rebellious Israelites. Yet God's gentle words are calling them back to Himself.

Can you hear His voice calling you? He longs to be gracious to you and to help you as you raise your children.

■ ■ ■

Am I trying to deal with my anger in my own strength and power?

Am I willing to turn to God for strength, wisdom, and self-control?

Seven Healthy Ways to Handle Anger

He who is slow to anger is better than the mighty,
And he who rules his spirit than he who takes a city.
—PROVERBS 16:32 NKJV

Anger is a God-given emotion
and in and of itself it is neither good or bad, right or wrong.
It's how we handle it and what we do with it that counts.
—DICK INNES

usan B. Anthony was angry because women were not allowed to vote, so she joined the effort toward women's suffrage. Rosa Parks was angry because she was treated differently due to the color of her skin, so she quietly made a stand from her seat on the bus. You are angry because your teenage daughter has started a pattern of showing you disrespect, so you choose an appropriate discipline and help her learn the importance of showing respect to others. Without a doubt, our anger can be used as a catalyst for a good, whether in our homes or in our nation.

Yet anger can also be destructive and ruin our relationships. Left unchecked, anger can eventually destroy everything important to us in life. The truth is, injustices will happen, people will hurt us, and situations will frustrate us or get us down. We will all face times when the emotion of anger wells up inside of us.

Perhaps you are steeped in anger right now. As I began writing this book, I became aware of some anger I didn't realize was lingering in my heart and mind. As I worked through my own anger, I used several of the healthy expressions described in this chapter. I can tell you from personal experience that this process helped me deal with my anger in a positive way, with beneficial results. Yes, my anger ended up working for the good because I handled it constructively instead of destructively.

> As you apply these seven healthy processes, you will begin to see your anger dissipate and eventually become minimal in your life.

In this chapter, you will find seven healthy ways to express your anger. Certainly there are more than seven, but these will help you begin to discover what may work for you. You may choose to use three or four of the forms of expression, or you may simply find that one works best for you. Pick and choose the solutions that fit your needs and your situation. Although each of the seven ways to express your anger is effective, you may find that anger keeps creeping back in your heart or mind. Don't be discouraged. Continue to prayerfully work through your anger in a healthy way. As you apply these seven healthy processes, you will begin to see your anger dissipate and eventually become minimal in your life.

Remember, you can head down a nonproductive road with your anger, or you can do something productive with it. Yelling and screaming fall into the nonproductive category. The silent treatment is also nonproductive and can lead to an explosion. So let's head down a productive road and explore seven healthy ways to resolve our anger with positive results.

Begin with Prayer

If we are going to look at our anger and squarely deal with it, we must begin with recognizing our need for the Lord's strength. It is difficult to direct the emotions of anger in a positive direction using simply our own strength and willpower. We need God's guidance step by step to help us deal with our emotions in a healthy way. As a gentle shepherd, the Lord can lead us down the pathway of healing our emotions and help us to handle them constructively.

As we pray, we are not necessarily looking to God to take away the circumstances or people at the root of our anger. We are asking Him to give us the wisdom and grace to deal with the situation or person. We seek His direction to lead us to wise solutions. Through prayer, we begin to take our eyes off the irritant and on to a great and mighty God who can heal broken hearts and smooth out bumpy roads. Prayer turns our eyes upward instead of inward in self-pity or outward in blaming someone else.

David said, "Have mercy on me, O LORD, for I am weak; O LORD, heal me, for my bones are troubled. My soul also is greatly troubled; but You, O LORD—how long? Return, O LORD, deliver me! Oh, save me for Your mercies' sake!" (Ps. 6:2–4 NKJV). Prayer is not a crutch to use as an excuse for our lack of self-control; rather, it is calling out to God, recognizing we need His strength, wisdom, and help to deal with our anger.

Healthy Solution #1: Pour Your Angry Energy into Positive Action

If we can turn our energy in a new direction and pour our thoughts and efforts into something positive, we will not only feel encouraged and uplifted but also our anger will significantly dwindle. So when you start to feel your anger rise, choose a productive, positive activity that will give you some sense of accomplishment or satisfaction and possibly work toward a solution.

When we turn our eyes toward doing a fresh positive activity, it takes the energy we want to pour into our anger and refocuses it for a good cause. Doing something positive and productive lifts our spirits, especially if we are lifting others up along the way. We always feel better about ourselves and our situation when we reach out to lend a helping hand or bless someone else, as we will discuss further in Chapter 13.

> Prayer is not a crutch to use as an excuse for our lack of self-control; rather, it is calling out to God, recognizing we need His strength, wisdom, and help to deal with our anger.

Recently, the news reported a story of a bride-to-be who found out six weeks before her wedding that her fiancé was being quite unfaithful. The wedding was painfully called off, but the bride's family had already reserved and paid for the wedding reception. So the bride decided to take this negative situation and make it into a positive. She chose two charities she wanted to support and invited guests to come to the reception, which was now turned into a fund-raising banquet. What a beautiful picture of turning the energy of anger and hurt into an uplifting blessing for others. Recognize the hurt, and then replace the anger with positive action.[1]

You may find that some of the following healthy activities help you work through your angry energy. Consider gardening, painting, writing, scrapbooking, cooking, reaching out to a new neighbor, walking, calling a friend, playing an instrument, reading a chapter of a book (even if you have to lock yourself in the bathroom to do so!), playing or coloring with the kids, reading a book to them, taking the kids to a movie or to the zoo, visiting a nursing home or invalid friend, or writing a note to lift someone else's day. Just make sure you are not suppressing your anger by turning toward these activities; rather, use them as a way to help you regain composure and work toward forgiveness.

Healthy Solution #2: Initiate an Honest and Loving Discussion

Never underestimate the power of an honest discussion. It can help build bridges instead of burning them and mend broken relationships instead of allowing them to grow apart. A good heart-to-heart can correct our false assumptions and can be a catalyst for positive change. I think we can all agree that a meaningful conversation between two people can help transform some of our ugly anger into a beautiful peace. Generally it is not the discussion that is difficult for us; it is the aspect of being loving and gracious during the discussion that seems to be the challenge.

I hate to admit it, but women often find it difficult to initiate an honest and loving discussion. When someone makes us angry (whether it is our spouse, in-laws, or our child's schoolteacher), our first reaction is to tell other people about our grievances. Now that does a lot of good, doesn't it? Instead of moving toward a productive solution, we repeat our frustration over and over again—and our anger festers and grows. The last thing on our minds is to discuss the issue with the person who has irritated or hurt us. So our anger eats us up inside every time we repeat it, while the other person has no idea we even have a problem.

Imagine the positive potential if we simply initiated a calm discussion with the person who has angered us. There would be less gossip and more productivity, less bitterness and more loving-kindness.

The apostle Paul wrote in his letter to the Ephesians, "Therefore each of you must put off falsehood and speak truthfully to his neighbor, for we are all members of one body. In your anger do not sin: Do not let the sun go down while you are still angry, and do not give the devil a foothold" (4:25–27). Paul recognized that we are going to get angry, but he tells us to go to the person who has offended us and speak truthfully with him or her instead of holding on to our anger and spreading it around. Do it soon; don't let your anger fester for days and become a huge issue. When we let things linger, we give the devil a foothold to destroy relationships and reputations.

> How do we get rid of our bitterness, rage, and anger? We begin by having a kind, compassionate discussion with the goal of benefiting the hearer.

Paul then tells us how to have a good, honest, and loving discussion. "Do not let any unwholesome talk come out of your mouths, but only what is helpful for building others up according to their needs, that it may benefit those who listen. And do not grieve the Holy Spirit of God, with whom you were sealed for the day of redemption. Get rid of all bitterness, rage and anger, brawling and slander, along with every form of malice. Be kind and compassionate to one another, forgiving each other, just as in Christ God forgave you" (Eph. 4:29–32). How do we get rid of our bitterness, rage, and anger? We begin by having a kind, compassionate discussion with the goal of benefiting the hearer.

Is there someone you need to call or meet with today? If so, I encourage you to put down this book right now and contact the person toward whom you feel anger. Ask the Lord to help you stay calm, respectful, and loving as you approach the person. Seek God's help to examine your own heart before you confront another. Also ask the Lord to allow the other person to be open to the discussion, and then leave the results in God's hands. You are not in charge of his or her response; you are simply responsible for sharing your concern lovingly and honestly. Try to work toward a positive solution, but remember there are times when you must agree to disagree. Most importantly, please stop sharing your grievances about the person with others; doing so is only destructive.

Healthy Solution #3: Journal Your Emotions

Journaling offers the opportunity to get your thoughts out of your head and onto paper. Your journal is a private place to pour out your heart. Journaling helps us recognize and release much of the emotions tangled up within our hearts and minds, even rumblings we didn't realize were there. If you continually struggle with anger, it is helpful to set aside a short time each day to write in your journal so that it becomes a habit or routine. Use your journal to write out prayers from your heart or wisdom you have learned throughout the day. Allow your thoughts and feelings to emerge, and don't worry about grammar or spelling or neatness.

Recognize the hurt, choose to forgive, make healthy changes, and move on.

Write out your angry emotions. Try to identify what is making you angry, whether it is a recurring situation that needs to be changed or someone or something that has hurt you in the past. Ask God to help surface the core of your hurt, pain, and anger. As you write, you may recognize that you need to talk with a mentor or a counselor about your anger and frustrations in order to work through the past and move on. If you notice you are rehashing the same old stuff over and over again, then you need to begin finding resolution through communication or change. Do not continue to wallow in the same angry issue. Recognize the hurt, choose to forgive, make healthy changes, and move on.

Healthy Solution #4: Find an Alternative Plan

Sarah's husband just couldn't seem to be on time for anything. When they met for lunch, he always arrived fifteen minutes late. When she flew back into town from visiting relatives, she was typically the last person at the baggage claim area, as he was usually late picking her up. They often had to take separate cars to church because he wasn't ready. He would eventually arrive at each destination—just not on time.

After numerous discussions and feeble attempts to convince him to change his ways, Sarah finally realized no matter how hard he tried, her husband wasn't ever going to arrive on time. Sarah had a choice. She could stew and boil over every time he was late, or she could accept the situation and choose to turn it into some sort of positive.

Sarah came up with a good solution. She loved to read, so she kept a good book with her at all times. When she found herself waiting for her husband, Sarah pulled out the book and caught up on some reading. She actually came to a point of hoping her husband would be late so she could finish another chapter. Sarah made a conscious decision to not allow her husband's habit of being late to take control over her emotions. She recognized this wasn't an issue worth getting worked up over, so she decided to stop focusing on his problem and see the situation from a new perspective.

When we are angry, we get our focus fixed on the irritant. A healthy expression of anger can be to take our eyes off the irritant and instead focus on creative solutions. Generally speaking, there is a way to work out most issues in a productive manner. Take little steps in a new direction. If you can't seem to see any alternatives, then talk to a trusted friend. Ask her to help you brainstorm new and better solutions, and then stop your bellyaching and move forward by trying an alternative plan.

Healthy Solution #5: Write a Letter

If there is a person who raises your dander, then write him or her a letter. Hold on now, I didn't say *send* the letter; I just said to write it. I strongly suggest you don't send the first draft of the angry letter you write. This letter is for your benefit rather than the recipient's. Get out a pen and paper and write down exactly what you would like to say to the person with whom you are angry. Let it pour out. Allow the issues that make you irate to flow from your heart and into the pen and onto the paper.

Go back and highlight what you consider to be the central issue or what is at the core of your anger toward this person. Can you identify one, maybe two things that are the hub of your anger?

> Coming to the place of forgiveness may take time, so be gentle with yourself.

Now I want to ask you to do something beyond your ability. I want you to ask God to help you forgive the person with whom you are angry. I know you may not be able to do this in your own strength and power, but God can help you begin to change your heart. Remember that we are all sinners and fellow strugglers in this journey. As Christians, we are recipients of God's mercy and grace. Coming to the place of forgiveness may take time, so be gentle with yourself. In Chapter 14, we will specifically address the process of forgiving others when you don't think you are able to do it.

If you still feel a need to express to the other person some of the issues in your letter, then I want you to write a new letter—one that is gracious and compassionate and will benefit the person who will receive it. Hold the letter for several days just to pray through and think through whether you should send it. You may find the passion of your anger has dissipated, so you want to write an even gentler letter or send nothing at all. You may also realize the best way to deliver the letter is in person, so you can read the letter to the person. Often it helps to read the letter aloud, so you can keep the facts straight as well as guard against emotions.

You will find the benefit of writing a letter allows an opportunity for underlying bitterness to surface and for you to decide if the issue is worth addressing or forgiving and moving forward.

Healthy Solution #6: Physically Work It Out

If you have angry energy, you can work it out of your system through a brisk walk or jog around the neighborhood or a hearty aerobics DVD at home. Often, a walk helps me clear my thoughts, regain composure, and work off the stress I've been carrying around in my body. When my kids were young, I would put them in the stroller and take them with me; other times I would wait until the evening when my husband could watch the kids. There are also many workout facilities that offer childcare. Explore your options. You may find it helpful to call a friend and create a plan where she can watch the kids for you while you take a walk or jog and vice versa.

A consistent exercise program can improve our mood and help reduce stress levels. The Better Health Channel reported, "Physical exertion burns up stress chemicals, and it also boosts production of mood-regulating neurotransmitters in the brain, such as endorphins and catecholamines."[2] These are some of the "feel good" hormones in your brain. You know yourself best, so choose an exercise routine that works with your schedule and your family responsibilities. Make a plan now; don't wait until it conveniently works into your schedule, or it probably won't happen. Regular exercise is good preventative medicine to help you keep your anger in check.

Healthy Solution #7: Talk to a Friend, Mentor, or Counselor

Sometimes we just need to vent. We need to pour out our hearts to a person who will listen and help us sort through the anger brewing in our hearts. That person may be a close friend, a relative, a mentor, or a biblically based counselor. Unless you have a very emotionally sensitive husband, I suggest that you not vent to him. The reason I say that is because often a husband is too close to the situation, he is not quite as feelings-oriented, and you may grow even more frustrated if he doesn't seem to understand. It is best to find a woman whom you can trust to hear you and give you a godly perspective. Talking to a friend can help us discern whether our anger is really worth it.

Mentors have been a blessing in my life. I particularly look for women who are mature in godly wisdom and with whom I can relate. Right now I know several women whom I can call anytime to ask for prayer and advice. We don't necessarily meet on a regular basis, but we get together now and then for coffee and spiritual encouragement. Where do you find a mentor? Begin with prayer, asking the Lord to bring someone into your life. Your church or local Bible study may be a good place to find that helpful relationship. Don't be afraid to reach out to a godly woman you respect and ask her if she would pray about beginning a mentoring relationship.

Friends and relatives can also offer wonderful means of support during times when we feel overwhelmed and full of anger. Perhaps a friend who has kids around the same age could be a good source of encouragement. Get the kids together to play while you talk through some of the issues on your heart. Again, sisters and friends can help us gain a fresh perspective, and sometimes our anger is softened just through the fact that someone has listened to us. Pent-up frustrations can lead to explosions, but simply telling another listening ear can help disarm some of those time bombs. I know in the early years of motherhood it may be difficult to get out of the house or be on the phone with other mothers and friends. Consider joining a MOPS (Mothers of Preschoolers) group or Hearts at Home or Early Childhood PTA group to find a connection with other mothers in your area.[3]

There may be a time when you feel overcome with anger to the point you want to seek professional help. If this describes you, I encourage you to see your doctor or find a biblically based counselor, perhaps one who has been recommended by other godly people you respect.

The Downside of Anger

Anger can also take a toll on our bodies. Numerous health problems are caused or worsened by unmanaged anger, including high blood pressure, headaches, digestion problems, skin problems, insomnia, increased anxiety, depression, heart attack, and stroke. Phew! The possible physical toll of anger is enough to make us want to stop mishandling it, but the consequences don't stop there. When not handled appropriately, our anger can lead to broken relationships, job loss, and harm to others. Mishandling our anger by suppressing it or exploding with it has life-altering consequences.

Don't ignore your anger. Recognize it, and begin to process it in a constructive way. Granted, expressing anger in a destructive way may seem to give you immediate gratification, but don't be fooled— people's lives (including your own) are destroyed in the wake. On the other hand, choosing to handle your anger in a wise and healthy way can bring positive results both for you and those around you. So before you explode or implode, employ one of the seven healthy ways to deal with your anger.

Love Notes from God

Show me the path where I should walk, O LORD;
point out the right road for me to follow.
Lead me by your truth and teach me,
for you are the God who saves me.
All day long I put my hope in you.

Remember, O LORD, your unfailing love and compassion,
which you have shown from long ages past.
Forgive the rebellious sins of my youth;
look instead through the eyes of your unfailing love,
for you are merciful, O LORD.

The LORD is good and does what is right;
he shows the proper path to those who go astray.

He leads the humble in what is right,
  teaching them his way.
The LORD leads with unfailing love and faithfulness
  all those who keep his covenant and obey his decrees.
(Ps. 25:4–10 NLT)

What path will we take with our anger? God can lead us down the right path of dealing with our anger. As He looks at us through the lenses of His unfailing love, He gently leads us.

Let us humbly come to Him, seeking His way and not our own. In our brokenness, as we recognize our anger, may we seek His help and direction in what to do with it. He knows us better than we know ourselves, and we can trust Him to faithfully direct our feet down the perfect path of healing from our anger and dealing with it in a healthy way.

■ ■ ■

What anger issue do I need to humbly lay before my heavenly Father?

Am I willing to trust His faithful love to lead me down the right path of dealing with my anger?

4

The Hidden Bs in Our Bonnets

Each heart knows its own bitterness,
and no one else can share its joy.
—Proverbs 14:10

If you are bitter at heart,
sugar in the mouth will not help you.
—Yiddish proverb

Not too long ago, we called an exterminator. We were certain that termites had invaded our home because there was an odd bulge protruding out of our dining room paneling. After careful examination both inside and outside our home, the pest-control man declared, "Mrs. Ladd, I've got good news and I've got bad news." *Uh-oh,* I thought. He continued, "The good news is you don't have termites. The bad news is I don't know what is causing the bulge. I've never seen anything like it."

His curiosity got the better of him, and he asked if he could try to discover the source of the problem. After thirty minutes he came in the house and said, "Mrs. Ladd, you aren't going to believe this. The bulge in your paneling is coming from the root from your crepe myrtle tree in your front yard. It made its way between the brick and the paneling and grew all the way up the inside of the wall." We couldn't believe it! The aggressive root had a life all its own. We eventually had to move the tree, yank out the renegade root, and repanel the area above the window in the dining room.

Have you ever heard of such a thing? I decided to look up crepe myrtles on the Internet to find out more about the root system. One article I read said that the root system of crepe myrtles "may be very hearty." Now that's an understatement! Those strong-willed monsters can do a heap of damage.

Did you know that the Bible warns us about a type of root system that can do lasting damage as well? They're not the kind of roots you find in your garden, but they are the kind you find in your heart. Hebrews 12:15 warns, "See to it that no one misses the grace of God and that no bitter root grows up to cause trouble and defile many."

Most of us do not deliberately choose to allow roots of bitterness or blame to grow in our hearts. But sometimes, without our even recognizing it, the seeds of bitterness are planted, take root, and begin to grow in our hearts. If left unattended, they begin to affect our relationships. In this chapter, we will examine how bitterness and blame creep into our lives, and then we will learn how to clean house so that these two pesky roots no longer take up residence in our hearts.

It Begins in the Brain

When I met Erica (not her real name), I was taken aback by her hardened demeanor. There was no way on this earth she was going to crack a smile, even though I greeted her with a sincere and warm hello. Erica seethed with bitterness and anger, and she made sure everyone around her knew it. Needless to say, she's not on the top of my list of people to call for a delightful little chat. If I am feeling low,

I probably won't call Erica to give me a lift. She seems pretty bent on staying in the pits. I have rarely met someone with such obvious bitterness and anger.

I've had quite a few revealing conversations with Erica that uncovered some of the roots of bitterness in her heart. There are certain circumstances in her life that have been a source of anger both at God and at certain family members. She has played the tapes of hurt over and over again in her head to the point that her anger has become as comfortable to her as old slippers or a favorite chair. Instead of dealing with her anger in a healthy way, she holds on to it like a prized possession. And that anger has overflowed into a cauldron of bitterness that affects every area of her life.

Our brains are continually at work storing new information as well as playing old files. If we choose to continue to pull out the "I am hurt" file and read it over and over again, we will eventually fill our lives with bitterness. What we must do instead is recognize the "I am hurt" file and then deal with it either by going directly to the source of hurt for a healthy discussion or by sincerely seeking to forgive the person.

In Erica's case, she felt as though it was her right to hold on to her "I am hurt" file; thus, she allowed it to become a root of bitterness that dominated her actions, words, and appearance. I believe secretly she hoped her bitter attitude would hurt those who hurt her, but the reality is her bitterness only hurts herself and her children.

Understanding Bitterness

Bitterness can be defined as "holding on to resentment or brooding over something a person did to hurt you." Bitterness typically is based on someone else's sin or wrongdoing (both imagined or real). It creeps in when you feel you have been wronged and lingers in your heart or mind if you choose to let it. Like the tree root in my house, bitterness is often unseen on the surface, yet it can grow rapidly and gain a stronghold in our lives.

The apostle Paul warns us to "get rid of all bitterness, rage and anger" (Eph. 4:31). The Bible doesn't leave the option open for us to dwell on our bitter thoughts. It is very clear that we must get rid of bitterness.

The first step in getting rid of our bitterness is to recognize it. We may be bitter toward God because He allowed a certain circumstance in our lives, or we may be bitter against a person who has wronged us. Although the issue seems to justify our bitterness, the fact is we must get rid of our bitterness, for it is only hurting us. Bitterness is not healthy, and it's not godly. James wrote, "But if you harbor bitter envy and selfish ambition in your hearts, do not boast about it or deny the truth. Such 'wisdom' does not come down from heaven but is earthly, unspiritual, of the devil" (3:14–15).

How do we recognize bitterness in our hearts? There may be some surface signals such as recurring thoughts of anger toward a certain person or constantly replaying what the person did to you in your mind. Another way to recognize bitterness is when you hear the person's name, you feel a desire for revenge. You may not be thinking about that person constantly, but when her name is brought up, you experience anger. Your bitterness may be against someone who is alive or against someone who has passed away. Your bitterness may even be against God.

Quit Pushing the Replay Button

In our house, my husband is in charge of the television remote control. Yes, it drives me nuts! It seems as if he's always switching channels just when I start to get interested in a program. Thank goodness someone else is not in control of the thoughts we play in our brains! No, that job is left totally up to us. We are in charge of the tapes we play in our minds. A thought from the past or a hurtful reminder of pain that we once felt may pop into our heads, but we don't have to dwell on it or replay it again and again in our minds. Yes, you've been hurt. So have I. We all have—it's part of life. Yet each of us must choose to stop replaying our pains, hurts, and frustrations.

> Recognizing our hurt or anger is good; replaying it over and over again isn't.

Recognizing our hurt or anger is good; replaying it over and over again isn't. We must deal with our hurt (through forgiveness and, perhaps, confrontation) and then move on.

In her article entitled "Yes, It Was Awful—Now Please Shut Up," Martha Beck encourages her readers to stop wallowing in self-pity and move forward in a positive direction. "As I obsess about my ancient problems, I feel more like I'm sinking in quicksand than lighting a torch. I'm creating neither heat nor light, just the icky, perversely pleasurable squish of self-pity between my toes. My only defense is that I'm not the only one down here in the muck—our whole culture is doting on tales of personal tragedy."[1]

Self-pity seems to be one of the hallmarks of today's society. Yet when our eyes are focused on "poor me"—on our own circumstances and problems—then the seeds of bitterness have fertile soil to grow. We must choose instead to turn our focus away from ourselves and move forward.

The apostle Paul encouraged Christians to play good tapes, not bitter ones, in their brains. "Finally, brethren, whatever things are true, whatever things are noble, whatever things are just, whatever things are pure, whatever things are lovely, whatever things are of good report, if there is any virtue and if there is anything praise-worthy—meditate on these things." (Phil. 4:8 NKJV). We can learn from the past and use our hurts to make us wiser and stronger, but we shouldn't continue to dwell on past pain.

Christian writer Fredrick Buechner says, "The sad things that happened long ago will always remain part of who we are just as the glad and gracious things will too, but instead of being a burden of guilt, recrimination, and regret that make us constantly stumble as we go, even the saddest things can become, once we have made peace with them, a source of wisdom and strength for the journey that still lies ahead."[2]

Let's choose to focus on the redemptive work God can do in our lives, instead of replaying what others have done to us. A quick glance at the Old Testament prophet Jeremiah gives us a powerful example of looking up to God instead of down in the mud. Jeremiah was hated and abused by people who didn't like his convicting message from the Lord. He was only doing what the Lord told him to do, yet he was thrown in a muddy pit as punishment. How unfair! But instead of focusing on the injustices done to him, Jeremiah placed his eyes on the goodness and power of what God could do. He said:

> I called on your name, O LORD,
>   from the depths of the pit.
> You heard my plea: "Do not close your ears
>   to my cry for relief."
> You came near when I called you,
>   and you said, "Do not fear."
>
> O Lord, you took up my case;
>   you redeemed my life.

You have seen, O LORD, the wrong done to me.

Uphold my cause! (Lam. 3:55–59)

Jeremiah chose to trust God's loving, sovereign plan. When we trust God's sovereignty, knowing that He sees all and can do all things, we begin to view our circumstances differently. We begin to ask, "Lord, what do You want me to learn through this circumstance or this person?"

The Danger of the Blame Game

"It's not my fault!" The blame game began in the Garden of Eden and continues until this day. Blaming others is a convenient way to take all the responsibility off ourselves and throw it on another person. Joan is negative and puts everyone down with her comments, but it's not her fault; if only she had had a mother who nurtured her. Tina has outbursts of rage with her kids, but it's not her fault; if only her husband would help her with the kids she wouldn't be so angry. Kathy is furious at her husband and shows it by her constant rudeness and disrespect, but it is not her fault; if only he would stop being so lazy and get a real job.

Who are you blaming for your negative behavior? Now, I'm not saying that you should ignore the frustrating circumstances. However, I am saying that you should do something positive toward a solution instead of coddling your anger and blaming others so you feel justified for it. Generally speaking, there are positive solutions to each negative situation, but a blame-game player doesn't want to look at the solutions. It's much too easy to float in the pool of "if-onlys" and coast down the road of "I can't help it; it's their fault." We are all good at the blame game, whether we are blaming our spouses, our bosses, our kids, our mothers-in-law, or even blaming God.

When we are busy throwing the blame on someone else, we fail to see our own sin and possible solutions or results of the situation. In Joan's case, she could work through the issues with her non-nurturing mom by recognizing that her mom is human and has faults and needs grace and forgiveness. Joan could focus on a good quality about her mom and also recognize that God can use the pain she feels to help her be a more compassionate person.

> When we are busy throwing the blame on someone else, we fail to see our own sin and possible solutions or results of the situation.

In the case of Tina, who is frustrated because her husband doesn't help her with the kids, she could create a logical plan of shared responsibility to discuss with him and solicit his help. If he is not willing or able to help with the children, then Tina needs to look for alternative solutions such as parents nearby or friends to trade off for help or hired help. Her first job is to declare that the blame game is over.

In the third scenario, Kathy could choose to stop treating her husband with rude disrespect and instead turn her focus toward his strengths and join with him to help him make the most of his career. Most men are strengthened and accomplish more when they have a woman who supports them and sees the best in them. Kathy could also look for a financial counselor to help them sort through their family's needs.

The point in each of these cases is there are typically solutions and possibilities to explore. Don't cozy up with blame and stay there. Move forward and find the solution that fits your situation. Yes, there may be a valid reason for your rage, anger, or rudeness. Use the source of agitation as a road sign to point you to a positive solution; don't use it as an excuse to blame someone else for your bad behavior.

Lose the Bitterness

How do we get rid of bitterness? Let's recap what we have learned.

- Recognize any bitterness you may be harboring in your heart.
- Trust God's love, wisdom, sovereignty, and redemptive power.
- Realize you may not understand His ways, but you can trust His love.
- Forgive the person toward whom you are harboring bitterness.
- Stop replaying the tapes of hurt and self-pity. Destroy the "I am hurt" file.
- Refuse to play the blame game.

We began this chapter by talking about the destructive roots of bitterness, but the Bible also talks about a beneficial root system. Colossians 2:7 says, "Let your roots grow down into him [Jesus] and draw up nourishment from him, so you will grow in faith, strong and vigorous in the truth you were taught. Let your lives overflow with thanksgiving for all he has done" (NLT). As we find our nourishment in Christ Jesus and what He has done for us, our roots grow deep in Him, not in people or circumstances.

We can grow a healthy root system by finding our nourishment in the eternal blessings of what God has done for us. And what has

He done for us? We can begin by reflecting on the loving act of sending His Son, Jesus, to this earth to die as a sacrifice for our sins. We no longer bear the burden and stain of our own sin. We are forgiven.

As our hearts overflow with thankfulness for our precious Savior, who offered His life so that we may be forgiven, we are able to begin forgiving others. As our roots are secure in Him, we begin to see that He has a plan and a purpose for our lives. Our pain can be used for a greater purpose. He can take the rubble other people have left in our lives and use it to create something beautiful. We may not understand why God allowed something to happen to us or why He allowed someone to hurt us, but we can trust that He loves us, is always with us, and sees the whole picture of our lives.

Love Notes from God

I am overcome with joy because of your unfailing love,
   for you have seen my troubles,
   and you care about the anguish of my soul.
You have not handed me over to my enemy
   but have set me in a safe place.

But I am trusting you, O LORD,
   saying, "You are my God!"
My future is in your hands.
   Rescue me from those who hunt me down relentlessly.
Let your favor shine on your servant.
   In your unfailing love, save me.

Your goodness is so great!
   You have stored up great blessings for those who honor you.

You have done so much for those who come to you for protection,
*   blessing them before the watching world.*
You hide them in the shelter of your presence,
*   safe from those who conspire against them.*
You shelter them in your presence,
*   far from accusing tongues.*
Praise the LORD,
*   for he has shown me his unfailing love.*
    (Ps. 31:7–8, 14–16, 19–21 NLT)

Oh the joy of God's unfailing love! Do you trust Him, my friend? God is sovereign. He sees our troubles and cares for the anguish of our souls. He has a bigger plan and can use even the bitter circumstances in our lives to bring about a sweet redemption. He is our advocate.

Are you willing to place your bitterness in His hands and leave it there? We will experience great joy and healing from our bitterness when we choose to place our trust in His unfailing love.

■ ■ ■

What "I am hurt" files am I harboring and replaying in my mind?

Am I willing to place this hurt in God's hands and seek solutions and healing?

5

Stopping the Mommy Explosion

Those who control their anger have great understanding;
those with a hasty temper will make mistakes.
—Proverbs 14:29 NLT

He who restrains his anger overcomes his greatest enemy.
—Latin Proverb

It was a good day. Tammy was up early and got herself and the kids dressed. She fixed their favorite breakfast and even had time for a third cup of coffee and a moment to spend reading her devotional before heading out the door to her favorite meeting of the month. It was her moms' meeting, where other mothers of preschoolers joined together to fellowship, hear a speaker, do a craft, and enjoy some mommy time.

As she was driving along, Tammy thought, *I'm so glad I bought those cute little outfits for the girls the other day. I'm sure the other moms will comment on how precious they look this morning.* The thought no sooner left her mind than she peeked in the rearview mirror and observed both girls pulling out their bows. They had already kicked off their shoes and socks. At the next stoplight, Tammy reached around to remedy the wardrobe situation and knocked over one of her daughter's cups, spilling its contents all over the car seat.

As she was trying to clean up the mess, the light turned green and the cars began honking behind her. "Just a minute!" she yelled at the cars. "Can't you see I've got a situation here!" She finally got the mess temporarily cleaned up and began driving. Unfortunately, her daughter began screaming, "Clothes wet! Off! Off!" and began squirming to take off her clothes.

"No!" Tammy yelled. "It's only a little juice. We can't be late for Mommy's meeting!" Tammy didn't have an extra pair of clothes for her, but her daughter continued screaming in the backseat. Tammy pulled over on a side street, stopped the car, and screamed above her daughter's screaming, "We are not going home! We will change clothes when we get home! Now stop crying and behave!" She gave them "The Glare" (you know, the one that could stop a raging bull).

> We may not be able to get rid of every mommy explosion, but we can be deliberate about reducing the possibility of losing it with our kids.

Both girls began crying. By now, Tammy was seething with anger. She wasn't sure if she was mad at her daughters or at the honking cars or at the fact that she was now late for the meeting (with dismantled outfits, no less). Maybe it was all of the above mixed into one big ball of frustration. *What happened?* Tammy thought. *The day started out so well, yet it's not even ten o'clock, and I've already lost it with the kids.*

Been there? We've all had those days. As a mom, every day has its own set of challenges. You never know what you're going to be facing. At times the frustrations, setbacks, spills, annoyances, hormones, and exhaustion can get the best of us, and like volcanoes we erupt. We didn't plan on it. We thought we were above exploding at our kids, but it happens.

We may not be able to get rid of every mommy explosion, but we can be deliberate about reducing the possibility of losing it with our kids. We can learn to deflect our anger and deal with it in a positive way so our words and actions do not have a negative or lasting effect on our children.

This is a practical chapter. First, we are going to identify your explosion triggers, and then we are going to look at ways to handle yourself in the heat of the moment. Finally, we are going to consider some preventative measures.

Please keep in mind, there is no one-size-fits-all solution when it comes to anger. Our angry explosions are typically based on our personalites and physical well-beings, to name just a couple of factors. As you read this chapter, look for the ideas that work best for you. My hope and prayer is you will find certain solutions in this chapter that will be a perfect fit to stop your fit.

Determining the Detonators

Let's begin by referring back to the anger self-assessment in Chapter 1. Flip back to the third section of the assessment (starting on page 13), concerning the triggers that set your anger in motion. Write down your top five triggers from that section in the space below. (Remember, don't let a friend borrow this book unless you tear out this page. This is personal stuff!)

Reasons or times I have lost it with my kids or husband:

_____

_____

_____

_____

_____

Now it is time to be a little more introspective. I want you to take each of the explosions you listed and write beside it what is the underlying personal issue. For instance, let's say the last time you lost it with your kids was when you were trying to get out the door on time for a meeting. Your underlying issue may be that you have a picture of perfection in your mind and you must maintain your "always-on-time" image. On the other hand, you may have difficulty organizing your time in the morning, or maybe you tend to oversleep. Be brutally honest with yourself. Humbly seek God's guidance as you open yourself up to recognizing any potential weaknesses or personal sin patterns.

> Humbly seek God's guidance as you open yourself up to recognizing any potential weaknesses or personal sin patterns.

As you look at your list of detonators to your mommy explosions and your own underlying issues, let's prayerfully move forward. Take each possible explosion and lay it before the Lord. First, confess to Him any sin you have realized as you have gone through this process. Please know He has forgiven the sin and moved on, and so must you (don't mentally beat yourself up here). Ask the Lord to heal any emotional pain experienced by your kids or husband due to your anger. Now humbly consider each issue before the Lord and ask Him if there are any preventative solutions.

Maybe you explode at your teenager because you are fearful she will go down the wrong path, so even a minor infraction makes you lose it. If so, a possible solution would be to place your fear of the future in God's hands while recognizing your screaming will not help your teen along the pathway of life. Instead, a good, healthy, sane discussion—when you have had a chance to calm down and pray about your fears—may be a positive personal solution. To tell you honestly, I don't have the exact answers for your solution, but God does! There may not be a practical or easy solution to every explosion, but we can choose to seek God's direction as far as the possibilities.

I can say from personal experience that when I ask God for wisdom on what to do, how to parent, or how to avoid an explosive situation, God is faithful to guide me in the right direction. One of my flustering problems is running late (no matter how early I get up), so my practical solution is setting my clocks five minutes ahead and writing down an earlier arrival time on my calendar.

Psalm 5:8 says, "Lead me in the right path, O LORD, or my enemies will conquer me. Tell me clearly what to do, and show me which way to turn" (NLT). This can be our prayer as well. As David did, we can ask God to lead us down the right path, so a potential explosion won't get the better of us.

Let's seek the Lord to show us solutions that lead us away from those underground mines. After a time of quiet prayer and reflection, write on the lines below the solutions God places on your heart for each of your five underlying personal issues.

_____

_____

_____

_____

_____

Keeping Your Cool When the Heat Is On

Like it or not, we are still going to encounter unforeseen times when we are about to boil over. Here are some on-the-spot ways to lessen the explosion. As you read through the following calmer-downers, find one or two practical ideas that will help you turn down your heat before a major explosion verbally annihilates all of your loved ones. Identify the solutions that fit where you and your kids are right now, and then come back and use other ideas as your kids get older.

The STOP Method. As you feel your temper temperature rising, remember the acronym *STOP.*

S stands for *step away from the situation.* Physically remove yourself from the immediate source of friction. It may mean stepping outside the room or the house for a moment. Of course, if you are at the store, do not leave your kids alone! But even there, take a few steps back from the immediate source of contention.

T stands for *take several deep, calming breaths.* Breathe deeply and give your body a chance to relax physically.

O stands for *objectively look at the situation.* Is this your hormonal time of the month? Are you hungry or tired? Are the kids hungry or tired? Is this an opportunity to train and discipline? If so, you will be much more effective by disciplining your children with wisdom and self-control rather than anger and screams.

P stands for *pray.* All of us need help from above to apply self-control. Cry out to your loving heavenly Father, who wants to help you. He loves your family, and He wants to help you. We may not have what it takes to stop the explosion with our own willpower, but when we recognize our dependence on our loving Father, we take a monumental step in the right direction. Praying turns our hearts and minds upward and reminds us that we are not alone.

The Wonder of a Whisper. Savvy schoolteachers know the power of a whisper. It takes energy to whisper, so take the energy you were about to pour into a scream and change it into a whisper. The kids have to pause to hear what you are saying. A whisper calms not only your spirit but also theirs. Use a gentle whisper, not a harsh one—yet say what needs to be said. However, I must warn you, don't overuse this approach as kids will grow callous to it.

Five-Minute Happy Vacation. Granted, you can't jump on the next plane to the Caribbean when you feel an explosion coming on, but you can take a short break from reality and do something that brings you a feeling of happiness. It may be flipping through a favorite magazine or relaxing in the easy chair for five minutes. If you have young kids or a lot of kids, you may need to announce that you are going to the bathroom just so you can have a short reprieve. Keep a favorite book, magazine, or catalog in there so you can take a short mental vacation. Just ignore the little fingers poking under the door!

Perhaps your happy time is playing with the dogs or doing a few stretches. It could be a short walk. It may not be a bad idea to ask one of the kids to give you a back massage. Maybe you find artwork or gardening or playing the piano to be a soothing vacation. Do it! Your kids will ultimately benefit from your brief times of respite.

In the space below, write down three personal, practical happy vacations you can take whenever you start to feel angry. Think about what makes you smile and what will honestly work in your life right now. Yes, you can come up with three! Keep thinking and praying; they will come to you. You will feel better just knowing you have these possible options.

_____

_____

_____

_____

Fresh Air and Sunshine. I don't know where you live, but if possible, step outdoors when you feel the rumblings of a mommy explosion. The wide-open space will help free you emotionally from those walls inside. Take several deep, lingering breaths of fresh air. Drink in the sunshine. Basking in the sunshine can raise the levels of happy hormones in your brain as your skin absorbs vitamin D. Studies now show that a dose of sunshine actually improves your mood. But be careful—not too much!

Change the Settings. If the noise is driving you nuts, then turn off the television, video games, or music, and enjoy the soothing silence. You may want to add some classical music to the room if you find it personally refreshing. If possible, gather the kids and go somewhere for a change of scenery. Simply moving the activities to a different room of the house can make a difference. For instance, if there is a battle over Barbies in the bedroom, then say, "Hey girls, let's all go to the kitchen to make some sandwiches." A change in venue, activity, or environment can be just the dose needed to help everyone go in a new direction.

Do a Necessary Reality Check. When you feel your anger level rising, ask yourself a very simple question: "Is this necessary?" If the kids are driving you insane with their fussing and whining at the mall, ask yourself, is it really necessary that you shop there today? If you are homeschooling your kids and everything is going wrong with everyone in the household, ask yourself, is it necessary to complete this lesson today, or can it wait until tomorrow? If the kids are scared to death of sitting on Santa's lap, then ask yourself, is it necessary to get the Santa picture this year? (The answer to that is no, by the way.)

Possibly one of the greatest phrases a mom can have in her arsenal is "Oh well." In other words, "Oh well, I guess we won't get all the laundry done today. Tomorrow is another day." "Oh well, so we didn't get to the park today." "Oh well, our gift is wrapped in newspaper because we couldn't find the wrapping paper. The wrapping will be thrown away anyway." I learned the "oh well" principle a long time ago from my dear friend Terry Ann, who has five kids. She survives with a smile because she lives the "oh well" philosophy and has learned how to do the necessary reality check.

Group Hug and a Good Laugh. I know it may seem simple, but sometimes all we need (or the kids need) is a hug. Coming together for a group hug helps us to refresh our loving hearts toward one another and relieves some of the tension in the air. A hug reminds us what our family is all about. Yes, we love our kids, and yes, we get annoyed at times. Do the actions and the feelings will follow. If you have momentarily lost that loving feeling for your husband or children, then wrap them in a warm embrace and watch your love feelings resurface.

> Do the actions and the feelings will follow. If you have momentarily lost that loving feeling for your husband or children, then wrap them in a warm embrace and watch your love feelings resurface.

Humor can also help defuse your anger. Now I'm not saying to laugh at your kids, but I am saying you may need to laugh with them at the situation instead of exploding in anger. One mom told me the story of her young son helping her bake cookies. When she left the kitchen to answer the door, she came back to find the kitchen and her son decorated with white flour. He said, "Look, Mom, fairy dust!" as he flung a handful of the flour.

Now, the mom had a choice at this point. She could have screamed in anger—or she could have laughed. Fortunately for all involved, she and her son laughed at the childhood foolishness and then worked together to clean up the mess. Of course, you need to be careful with laughter, as you don't want to give your kids the impression that what they are doing is cute. Teach and train your children wisely, but be ready to defuse the tension through laughter at the right moment.

Preventative Measures

Just as our cars need maintenance in order to run smoothly, so moms need a little preventive maintenance to help us run smoothly and to protect us from boiling over. Here are some thoughts to help you have a smoother ride through the challenges of motherhood.

Take Care of Your Body. Your physical well-being plays a big part in your ability to handle stress. It's important for every mom to take a good multivitamin every day, so pretend I'm your mom right now asking, "Did you take your vitamin today?" Do it, as it will help you and strengthen your emotional as well as physical stamina.

Are you eating right? We need to fuel our bodies with foods that will strengthen us. Increase your intake of fruits, veggies, whole grains, and lean protein. Reduce or eliminate sugar, white flour, and trans fats. Drink lots of water, and if you find that you are on edge all the time, you may want to reduce your caffeine intake as well.

Have you seen your doctor lately? Certain medical factors, such as hormone imbalance or thyroid deficiency, can cause mood swings and irritability. After giving birth to her second child, my friend Jennifer noticed an increased irritability, combined with other symptoms such as exhaustion and hair loss. A visit to her OB confirmed that, like many breastfeeding moms, she had a thyroid deficiency. Once she started taking her thyroid medication, her mood improved dramatically! So if you are experiencing sudden mood swings or irritability, I encourage you to discuss it with your doctor.

And one more thing, are you getting enough rest? If you have an infant or toddler, getting a good night's sleep may be difficult, but do try to nap when the kids are napping if you can. And try to go to bed at a reasonable time in the evenings.

Okay, enough mothering, but I had to say it!

Don't Overcommit Your Family's Time. Maxing out our schedules is easy to do. There are so many great opportunities for both you and your kids. Guard your schedule like a mother bear! You don't have to do everything just because everyone else is doing it. Do what is right for your family. A calm, gentle, and happy mom is much more effective than a busy, frazzled, overinvolved mom. Prayerfully commit your schedule to God, and carefully consider the long-term benefits or damage of time-consuming teams and activities.

> A calm, gentle, and happy mom is much more effective than a busy, frazzled, overinvolved mom.

Schedule Time with Friends and Other Moms. Never underestimate the positive power of a friend! Sharing your war stories and being encouraged by another person can have a positive impact on your emotional well-being. If you don't have a friend whom you can confide in right now, I encourage you to reach out. Look for a moms' group at your local church. As I mentioned in Chapter 3, Mothers of Preschoolers (MOPS), Hearts at Home, and Early Childhood PTA all provide wonderful opportunities for friendships with other moms. You can also find new friends at the park or by getting involved in your kids' school or local homeschooling association. Call a friend at least once a week for a heart-to-heart, encouraging chat.

Once-a-Month Gift to Self. Remember the "happy vacation" idea discussed in the last section? Well, now I want you to think of something that would be a gift to yourself if someone else watched the kids for an hour. Each month, schedule one hour for someone else to watch the kids while you are going to give yourself a little gift. Yes, indulge yourself! It may be a bubble bath, a manicure, a massage, or an hour in a bookstore or a coffee shop. What is your pleasure? You can afford to be away from your kids for one hour a month, I know you can. So write it on your schedule, and make it something you will look forward to. When you are feeling frustrated or overwhelmed, you have your "gift to self" to look forward to each month.

Help Options. Mother's Day Out, housecleaning, yard service, or help from the in-laws all can be welcome relief at times. My friend Becky became a new person the day she hired a cleaning service to help with her home and laundry once a week. With two preschoolers and a new baby, having the extra help took the edge off for her.

Please don't feel guilty for doing something that will help you be more pulled together as a mom. If you are not able to afford these options, then see if you can barter or trade off time with a friend. We all need help at times. Examine your life and what seems to be overwhelming you, and seek out the assistance you need.

Dancing Around the Land Mines

What is the key to stopping your mommy explosion? I can't answer that; only you can. Using the ideas in this chapter, personalize your solution to fit who you are and what your life is like right now. The honest truth is, life isn't perfect, kids aren't perfect, your husband isn't perfect, and neither are you. We all are fellow strugglers. We can't go through life dancing around potential land mines, hoping we don't explode. We must recognize that every day presents its own set of land mines in the form of mistakes, unforeseen challenges, and simple frustrations.

We must remain flexible to the detours each day presents and employ the practical tips in this chapter. Recognize each day is a new day, and determine to handle annoyances and irritations with a peaceful response instead of an out-of-control reaction. Self-control and peace are two attributes that do not come naturally to us, but they do to God. They are fruits of His Spirit.

I encourage you to start each day with a simple prayer like this:

Wonderful, loving heavenly Father, I don't know what this day holds, but I know You hold me by the hand. Lead me, guide me, and give me the patience and strength I need for this day. Let Your peace rule my heart. In Jesus's name, amen.

Love Notes from God

Bless the LORD, O my soul;
And all that is within me, bless His holy name!
Bless the LORD, O my soul,
And forget not all His benefits:
Who forgives all your iniquities,
Who heals all your diseases,
Who redeems your life from destruction,
Who crowns you with lovingkindness and tender mercies,
Who satisfies your mouth with good things,
So that your youth is renewed like the eagle's.

The LORD executes righteousness
And justice for all who are oppressed.
He made known His ways to Moses,
His acts to the children of Israel.
The LORD is merciful and gracious,

Slow to anger, and abounding in mercy.
He will not always strive with us,
Nor will He keep His anger forever.
He has not dealt with us according to our sins,
Nor punished us according to our iniquities.

For as the heavens are high above the earth,
So great is His mercy toward those who fear Him;
As far as the east is from the west,
So far has He removed our transgressions from us.
As a father pities his children,
So the LORD pities those who fear Him.
For He knows our frame;
He remembers that we are dust. (Ps. 103:1–14 NKJV)

God knows us. He loves us. He helps us. He forgives us. What a wonderful God we serve! His mercy toward us will never cease. As fellow moms, let us continually reflect on His love and be renewed by His grace.

Seek God's help when you are in the pit of despair, turn to Him when you feel weak, and run to Him when you feel guilty. His arms are loving and strong.

■ ■ ■

Which of the qualities of God listed in this passage give me hope and strength as a mom?

6

"I Can't Believe I Just Said That!"

A soft answer turns away wrath,
But a harsh word stirs up anger.
The tongue of the wise uses knowledge rightly,
But the mouth of fools pours forth foolishness.
—PROVERBS 15:1–2 NKJV

Speak when you are angry
and you'll make the best speech you'll ever regret.
—HENRY WARD BEECHER

Joni wanted to scream! She finally had all the kids clothed and with shoes on, hair combed, and ready to leave the house—and then it happened.

Five-year-old Ashley was only trying to help Mommy by preparing little Katherine's juice cup. Ashley had watched her mom pour the juice from the pitcher many times, and she just knew she could do it too. *Mommy will be so proud that I helped her,* Ashley thought. Unfortunately, Ashley's act of service turned into a major disaster. As you've probably already guessed, the pitcher was too heavy, Ashley dropped it, and juice and shattered glass went everywhere.

"What are you doing? You just weren't thinking, were you? I can't believe you made this mess! Now we are going to be late to my meeting, and it is all your fault! How could you do something so stupid!"

Oh my, quite a lot for a five-year-old to bear. Ashley's little spirit was crushed, and "Mommy's little helper" had all of her confidence drained right out of her with just a few angry comments made in the heat of the moment. Do you think Ashley will try to help or try anything new for a while? Not as long as she still has the memory of her mommy's harsh words rolling around in her head.

> **Our words are powerful. They can be used to give courage and strength, or they can be used to dash confidence and drain hope.**

Our words are powerful. They can be used to give courage and strength, or they can be used to dash confidence and drain hope. As moms, we want our words to be a gift to our families, delicious morsels that nourish each family member. Sometimes in the heat of the moment or in the midst of frustration, hurting words emerge from our mouths. How can we possibly gain control of the dangerous monster known as the tongue?

Taming the Tongue

If you are reflecting on all the awful things you have said to your kids, you are not alone. You are joined by the entire human race, for no one is above saying things they regret. Foot-in-mouth disease is rampant; we've all experienced it more often than the common cold.

Even the Bible reminds us how difficult it is to tame the tongue. Here's what James had to say:

> We all make many mistakes, but those who control their tongues can also control themselves in every other way. We can make a large horse turn around and go wherever we want by means of a small bit in its mouth. And a tiny rudder makes a huge ship turn wherever

the pilot wants it to go, even though the winds are strong. So also, the tongue is a small thing, but what enormous damage it can do. A tiny spark can set a great forest on fire. And the tongue is a flame of fire. It is full of wickedness that can ruin your whole life. It can turn the entire course of your life into a blazing flame of destruction, for it is set on fire by hell itself.

People can tame all kinds of animals and birds and reptiles and fish, but no one can tame the tongue. It is an uncontrollable evil, full of deadly poison. Sometimes it praises our Lord and Father, and sometimes it breaks out into curses against those who have been made in the image of God. And so blessing and cursing come pouring out of the same mouth. Surely, my brothers and sisters, this is not right! Does a spring of water bubble out with both fresh water and bitter water? Can you pick olives from a fig tree or figs from a grapevine? No, and you can't draw fresh water from a salty pool. (James 3:2–12 NLT)

Whew! After reading the passage above you may feel defeated, thinking there is literally no way to tame your tongue. It's true that we can't tame our tongues, but with God all things are possible; so don't lose hope. Let's look at ways to put a harness on one of the wildest of creatures ever created, the human tongue.

The Origin of Our Words

Perhaps you have been surprised at times by the negative words that have come out of your mouth. I know I have. It may start with one or two slips of unkind accusations toward our kids or husbands. Then we grow more comfortable with our angry and unruly tongues. It could be that your mother used unkind and demeaning words, and now you have picked up the habit. Unfortunately, we begin to think our underhanded remarks or cutting comments are no big deal, not recognizing the lasting damage our words are doing to others. If no one calls us on the carpet or admonishes us about our tongues, our hurtful words or tones slowly become a habit.

Most of us can recall childhood incidents where someone's unkind remarks hurt us deeply and left a lasting scar. We must realize that our words weigh heavy on young hearts and minds, so we must get to the root of the problem and choose to make positive changes.

> We must examine what is in our hearts, for the treasures in our hearts spill out into our words.

Where do our harsh and hurtful words come from? Let's look first at what the Bible says. Jesus explained that our words are an outflow of the heart. Here is what He said to the Pharisees: "For out of the abundance of the heart the mouth speaks. A good man out of the good treasure of his heart brings forth good things, and an evil man out of the evil treasure brings forth evil things" (Matt. 12:34–35 NKJV).

Think of it this way: a jostled cup will spill over with the substance with which it is filled. There have been mornings when I grabbed a to-go cup of coffee and jumped into the car, rushing off to a meeting or appointment. Unfortunately, on more than one occasion, the coffee has sloshed out of the cup and onto my clothes. At that point I wish my cup had only been filled with water. A slosh of water does very little damage and soon dries, but a slosh of hot coffee not only burns but also stains.

I'm sure you'd agree that we want our words to be more like cleansing, refreshing water than burning, staining coffee. Therefore, we must examine what is in our hearts, for the treasures in our hearts spill out into our words. We all struggle with our mouths because each one of us struggles with sin. Let's recognize our humble need for God's help to change our hearts and create in us clean hearts. As David said, "Let the words of my mouth and the meditation of my heart be acceptable in Your sight, O LORD, my strength and my Redeemer" (Ps. 19:14 NKJV).

Filling Our Cups with Good

How do we fill our hearts and minds with pure water rather than scalding, staining coffee, so to speak? I honestly believe we begin to fill our hearts with good treasures by choosing to focus our minds on positive things rather than negatives. Have you been focusing on negative, frustrating, or depressing areas? It's time to weed out some of these downers and replace them with uplifting thoughts.

Praise God for who He is and thank Him for what He has done. Join King David in saying, "I will bless the LORD at all times; His praise shall continually be in my mouth" (Ps. 34:1 NKJV). As we fill our hearts with praise for God's wonderful attributes, our mouths can't help but overflow with praise.

I encourage you to begin each day with praise. As you turn off the alarm or hold your crying baby in the early morning hours, turn your heart toward praise.

Praise Him for His loving-kindness.

Praise Him for His mercy.

Praise Him for His sovereignty.

Praise Him for His goodness.

Praise Him for being your Good Shepherd.

Praise Him for being sufficient to meet your needs.

Praise Him for creating the universe.

Praise Him for knowing all things.

Praise Him for His ability to do all things.

Praise Him for being with you always and never leaving you.

There now, did that help you get started? Reflecting on God's goodness is a wonderful way to start your day and fill your heart with good treasures. Develop the habit of praise every morning, and you will find your heart overflowing with joy for who God is. Praising God fills our thoughts with the greatness of God and gets our hearts and minds off of some of the negative thoughts that tend to defeat us.

In his letter to the Colossians, the apostle Paul encourages believers to allow God's peace to rule our hearts and to let Christ's words dwell in us richly. Notice how many times in this short passage he mentions giving thanks.

And let the peace that comes from Christ rule in your hearts. For as members of one body you are all called to live in peace. And *always be thankful.*

Let the words of Christ, in all their richness, live in your hearts and make you wise. Use his words to teach and counsel each other. Sing psalms and hymns and spiritual songs to God *with thankful hearts.* And whatever you do or say, let it be as a representative of the Lord Jesus, *all the while giving thanks* through him to God the Father. (3:15–17 NLT; emphasis added)

By thanking God, we fill our lives with refreshing water. Not sure where to begin thanking God? We can always begin at the Cross. Thank God for sending Jesus to pay the penalty for your sin. Thank Him that Jesus rose from the dead, giving you hope of eternal life. Thank Him that through faith you are a part of His family and a partaker of His glorious grace. Thank Him for the gift of the Holy Spirit, who is with you and able to work in a mighty way in your life.

Every day I find it helpful to return to the basics of faith by thanking God for my salvation. This keeps me coming back to my first love and the joy of knowing Him. Of course, our thankfulness to God can extend to all the blessings in our lives.

Begin with the people in your life, thanking God for their good qualities (and yes, everyone has some quality about which you can thank God). Continue by thanking God for all the blessings He has brought into your life, whether big or small. Make it a practice to go to sleep at night thanking the Lord for all He has done. As you lay your head on your pillow, allow thankful thoughts to send you off to sleep. If you develop the habit of praising God in the morning and thanking Him as you go to sleep, your heart will be filled with glorious treasures that overflow through your mouth.

> When we hide God's Word in our hearts, it begins to overflow in our words as well.

We could take a lesson from David, a man after God's own heart, who declared, "It is good to give thanks to the LORD, and to sing praises to Your name, O Most High; to declare Your loving-kindness in the morning, and Your faithfulness every night" (Ps. 92:1–2 NKJV).

A Rich Wellspring from Your Heart

Did you notice another heart principle in our earlier passage from Paul? He said, "Let the words of Christ, in all their richness, live in your hearts and make you wise" (Col 3.16 NLT). There is a rich blessing in filling our minds with the beautiful truths that are found in His Word. As we read and meditate upon Scripture, our hearts fill with love for God.

Have you ever noticed when you truly love someone, you begin to reflect some of his qualities? I know throughout the years in my marriage, I have grown to enjoy many of the same activities and interests Curt likes. In a similar way, as we fall in love with Christ and draw close to Him, we begin to reflect His qualities. When we hide God's Word in our hearts, it begins to overflow in our words as well. I have found that as I memorize God's Word and have it continually on my mind, it tends to roll off my lips.

How do we fill our minds with God's Word as busy moms? There are several ways you can do it and bless your families as well. One way is by listening to Scripture on CDs. You can buy CDs of Scripture verses put to delightful, catchy tunes at almost any Christian retailer. After you listen to the songs, the Scripture verses often linger in your mind all day long.

> A gentle and wise response to an offense has a powerful effect.

Another helpful tool is a book called the *Well Versed Family*, written by my friend Caroline Boykin. In it you will discover creative ways to teach memory verses to your kids, and you will learn them as well. Caroline's book is written out of her own experience of teaching her kids to hide God's Word in their hearts, and it is an excellent tool for every mom.

Many times, I write down memory verses on index cards. I ask the Lord to lead me to passages I need to memorize, then I take my index cards with me when I go on walks in the morning and keep them with me throughout the day. I like to practice old verses and learn new ones as I walk.

Are you afraid to embark on Scripture memory because you think you can't do it? Ask God not only to lead you to the passage you should memorize but also to help you memorize it. He desires for you to have His Word dwelling in you richly, so that it will over-flow in your words.

David said, "With my whole heart I have sought You; oh, let me not wander from Your commandments! Your word I have hidden in my heart, that I might not sin against You" (Ps. 119:10–11 NKJV). As we fill our hearts and minds with the purity and power of God's Word, we will begin to see a change in what flows from our mouths. No, it is not a guarantee that we will never say another harsh word, but it is a giant step in the right direction as we fill our cups with living water.

Refreshing Water

Solomon said, "A person's words can be life-giving water; words of true wisdom are as refreshing as a bubbling brook" (Prov. 18:4 NLT). Let's think of our words as an opportunity to refresh our kids. It is vital for us to recognize the power of our words. They can be a life-giving tool or a damaging one. Our kids need refreshing, help-ful words to teach and admonish them. When our kids make a mis-take or do something wrong, we need to use our words as a bandage to help them heal, using wise and helpful discipline.

Wise words of correction can help our kids to grow, while harsh words stir up anger. Kind, life-giving words train and teach. Angry, screaming, cruel words only serve to hurt and scare. Oh sure, our loud, stinging words may change our child's behavior for the day, but there is no telling how those words may damage him for life, stealing his confidence, stirring his anger, making him feel as though he will not amount to anything.

Let's think about a situation that may stir up harsh words. Let's say your ten-year-old son has just walked in the house with muddy shoes. Now think about what you would like to say. ("I told you a hundred times to take off your shoes before coming in the house! Now look what you've done! You just don't think, do you?")

Don't say that! Instead, think about what response will lead to correction and a better human being. Give him a drink of water. "Son, please turn around and look behind you. Would you please take off your shoes? Now I need you to get a rag from the kitchen and clean this up immediately." You may want to gently add the fact there will be a harsher consequence if this happens again, such as cleaning the entire house or taking away his favorite shoes for a week.

> Our kids learn how to respect us and others as they learn from our example.

A gentle and wise response to an offense has a powerful effect. It not only changes behavior but also builds a better person. Our kids are learning how to respond in heated situations through our examples. Do we want them to learn to scream and shout to accomplish their goal, or do we want them to learn how to handle a situation with dignity and honor? Continually recognizing the power of our words can help us curb our verbal barrage. Let's keep in the forefront of our hearts and minds that we want our words to be refreshing and life giving, not berating.

Let me address the subject of sarcasm here. Some mothers may take pride in never raising their voices in anger to their kids, yet their sarcastic remarks can be equally cruel. The use of sarcasm is demeaning and belittling to the victim. It is easy to grow into the nasty habit of using it without recognizing the damage it causes. Responding to your child's question with, "Well, duh," can make him feel stupid. We want our words to bring grace, not hurt, to our children.

If you struggle with remembering the power of your words, I

suggest writing the following question on an index card and posting it on the refrigerator or in the car—wherever you need it: "Are my words as refreshing as life-giving water?" Remember, our kids are thirsty for encouragement, wisdom, and discipline. May our words be a cup of refreshing water to our children as we lovingly teach and discipline them.

Let's Be Honest

Owning up to our own unkind words is half the battle. When we come clean and choose to be honest with ourselves and with God, we begin to head down the road of healing. We all struggle with our words to some extent. Let's get that out on the table and in humility come before the Lord, confessing our need for forgiveness and help. Whether it is demeaning words we whisper under our breath or cutting words we shout in the heat of the moment or even just a rude way of saying something, we each need to recognize our personal weaknesses and seek God's forgiveness and strength.

It may be helpful to make a list of words you tend to use that are degrading toward others and you know you shouldn't say. Just as you tell your kids certain words are off limits, you must determine these words are off limits to you. Sometimes it is not what you say but how you say it. The words *Oh really?* can be taken several different ways according to the intonation of your voice. Consider the importance of respect not only in your words but also in your tone of voice. Your kids learn how to respect you and others as they learn from your example.

It may be difficult to see the way our words cause pain in others. Ask the Lord to reveal to you the ways your words may have hurt your family in the past. You may even want to ask your family members to tell you of times in the past when you have hurt them with your words. This could be a painful process, but one that will allow you to open lines of communication with your family. This may also give you an opportunity to apologize and bring healing to some past hurts or bitterness that could be taking root in your family. God can use our humility and brokenness to move our families to a new level of love.

If you are battling a hurtful tongue, please consider confessing it not only to the Lord but also to a friend who can pray for you and hold you accountable. I know this is a hard suggestion because we don't want anyone to know our dirty little sins of the mouth. Yet confessing our faults and weaknesses to a wise and godly friend can help bring us to a place of renewal. Choose carefully the person with whom you will share the secrets of your heart. Enjoy the blessing of being strengthened by a friend because as iron sharpens iron, one woman can sharpen another (see Proverbs 27:17).

A Gentle Process

Please don't spend time fretting about the words you have already let spill out of your mouth. Apologize if necessary. Recognize God is able to heal past wounds. He is also able to give you what you need. Remember, the tongue is a tough animal to tame. We must recognize our weakness and turn to God. One of the fruits of His Spirit is self-control, along with other fruits such as love, peace, gentleness, and kindness (see Galatians 5:22). Even if you grew up in a home where unkind words flowed freely, God can free you from the bonds of the past and make you a new creation. Seek God and ask His help in overcoming your past and starting a new cycle of positive, healing words for the next generation.

As we review what we learned in this chapter, I think our most important lesson is to depend on the Lord. We need His help day by day. We also learned the importance of filling our hearts with praise and filling our minds with God's Word. In order to have good words flow out of us, we must fill ourselves with good words and truth. As we continue to grow in the knowledge of His Word and hide it in our hearts, we grow in wisdom and purity—and our tongues become refreshing rather than hurtful. We must also recognize the immense power of our words and see them as a tool for training and healing, not whipping someone into submission.

> Seek God and ask His help in overcoming your past and starting a new cycle of positive, healing words for the next generation.

I hope you now see your words as powerful and potentially life giving. Our words can be used for teaching, encouraging, and building, just as much as they can be used for hurt, pain, and destruction. May we guard our hearts and our lips so we may glorify God in what we do and say.

Proverbs 22:11 says, "Anyone who loves a pure heart and gracious speech is the king's friend" (NLT). When it comes to motherhood, anyone who loves a pure heart and gracious speech is a blessing to her family. Wouldn't you agree?

Love Notes from God

I will repay you for the years the locusts have eaten—
the great locust and the young locust,
the other locusts and the locust swarm—
my great army that I sent among you.
You will have plenty to eat, until you are full,

and you will praise the name of the LORD your God,
  who has worked wonders for you;
never again will my people be shamed.
Then you will know that I am in Israel,
  that I am the LORD your God,
  and that there is no other;
never again will my people be shamed. (Joel 2:25–27)

Oh, how dearly loved we are by God! He is a restoring and redeeming God. This passage refers to a time when Israel was rebellious and God told them their crops would completely be destroyed by locusts. But as surely as their sins had consequences, the Lord also assured His people that as they turned to Him, He would redeem the years the locusts had eaten.

Yes, God knows our faults, but He can also heal the messes we have made. Let's turn to Him and seek His help to walk in His ways. He is faithful and able to do wonders far beyond what we could ask or imagine.

■ ■ ■

Am I willing to change direction and ask God to help me guard my mouth?

In what areas do I need to seek His healing for the past wounds I have caused to others?

Learn How to Respond to Their Anger

Live in harmony with each other. Don't try to act important, but enjoy the company of ordinary people. And don't think you know it all! Never pay back evil for evil to anyone. Do things in such a way that everyone can see you are honorable. Do your part to live in peace with everyone, as much as possible.

—Romans 12:16–18 NLT

Anger is just one letter short of danger.

—Vern McLellan

We can extinguish many family fires by responding wisely to our family members' anger rather than simply reacting to it.

7

What to Do With a Crying Baby

You have taught children and nursing infants to give you praise.
—Psalm 8:2 NLT

Adam and Eve had many advantages,
but the principal one was that they escaped teething.
—Mark Twain

ou've prepared for almost nine months for an eagerly anticipated new member of your family. The nursery is decorated
and stocked with baby clothes and diapers, and your family and
friends are overjoyed. It's all so wonderful! That is, until you come
home from the hospital and your baby begins to cry and you can't
figure out how to console him. Motherhood is not quite as easy and
blissful as you may have anticipated. Isn't it amazing how this precious new addition to the world, so tiny and sweet and innocent, has
the power to fluster and frazzle you simply by crying?

Your little treasure from God is not deliberately trying to frustrate you, although it may feel that way sometimes. A crying baby is
simply trying to communicate the only way he can. No matter how
frustrating the crying may be, we need to remember that our baby's
intent is not spiteful, but rather based on need, comfort, and survival.

A mother's response to her baby's cries can reassure him and give him a sense of security. "Picking up and attending to your crying baby won't spoil her. For the first few months, you are getting to know your baby and she is getting used to being in the world," says pediatrician Maud Meates-Dennis. "By being responsive to her crying you are letting your baby know that she is loved and cared for and that will give her security."[1]

A newborn baby may cry for more than two hours on any given day. As you get to know your baby, you will begin to figure out why she is crying—perhaps she is hungry or tired or in need of a diaper change. It also helps to know some practical techniques to calm the crying and cope with the tears. Let's begin by examining some of the reasons babies cry and then some creative ways to deal with it.

Why Do Babies Cry?

Babies must rely on someone else to provide for their basic needs of comfort, warmth, and food. Typically when a baby cries, he is trying to communicate a specific need. As a new mom, you may be frustrated by your baby's cries as you desperately try to figure out what could be upsetting your precious little one. Gradually, you will begin to recognize your baby's patterns as you get to know his needs. Let's examine some of the reasons a baby cries.

Hunger. The most common reason a baby cries is because he needs to be fed. If it has been more than three hours since he last ate, he may be hungry again. Most newborns eat every few hours (unfortunately around the clock), with the exception of the first day or two after birth when some babies feed very little. Some babies may get so upset when they are hungry that by the time they begin feeding, they gulp air with the milk—which causes them to spit up or cry even louder.

Try to gently calm your baby before feeding him, and if your baby begins to gulp, take a short break. Take time to burp your baby during and after each feeding. Your baby may need to be burped between meals as well.

Diaper Change. Some babies become especially upset when their diapers are soiled or wet while other babies seem perfectly content even when they have a full diaper. Check your baby's diaper often to make sure it is dry. Also, check the tabs to make sure the diaper fits properly and the tabs are not irritating his skin.

Need to Be Comfortable. Babies often cry if they are too hot or too cold. Touch your baby's stomach to feel if he is too hot or too cold (feeling hands or feet is not a good guide as they usually feel slightly colder). Add a layer of clothing or take one away accordingly. Your baby may feel more secure or comfortable bundled in a swaddle wrap, which is explained in the next section.

Tiredness. A tired baby can be a fussy baby. If you notice your baby losing interest in people or toys, rubbing his eyes, yawning, or decreasing activity, he may need a nap. If you respond early to your baby's cues of tiredness, you may avoid a major outburst of tears.

Newborns need up to sixteen hours (or more) of rest each day, so make sure your baby is getting the sleep he needs. Sometimes your baby may be overstimulated due to a busy day or lots of people around, so you will need to take him to a quiet, dark place away from the stimulation in order to get some rest.

Need to Be Held. Many babies need an extra dose of cuddling and reassurance that you are there. Newborns especially need close physical contact for comfort, whereas older babies may be reassured by seeing or hearing their parents nearby. The Mayo Clinic reports,

"Babies who are held or carried during most of their waking hours are less fussy than those left in a crib or infant seat."[2] You may find a baby sling helpful, allowing you to keep your baby close while freeing up your hands. A gentle massage or light pats on the back also reassure your baby through your touch.

Overstimulation. Too much activity, too many people, or too much noise may be too much for a baby. If you notice your baby shutting his eyes or turning his head and crying, he may be trying to shut out all the stimuli around him. This would be a good time for a change in scenery, perhaps moving to a dark, quiet room; or if the weather is nice, it may be good to head outdoors for some peace and quiet and fresh air. A calmer environment and maybe even some gentle white noise like a ceiling fan could help your baby calm down.

Pain or Illness. If you have checked the above motivations and your baby is still crying, you may want to explore the possibility that he is in pain or ill. A baby who is sick or in pain often cries in a different tone than his normal cry. It could be sudden and shrill or higher pitched.

Check your baby's temperature and do a full examination of his body to make sure there are no rashes or obvious problems. Make sure his clothes are not too tight or pinching him. If your baby is at least three months old, you might also want to run a clean finger along his gum line to see if his gums are swollen or if you can feel a tooth coming through. If so, you can offer him a refrigerated (not frozen) teething ring or obtain your pediatrician's permission to use an over-the-counter oral anesthetic such as Oragel.

Some babies have a reaction to certain kinds of formula. If you are breastfeeding, your baby may be reacting to spicy or gas-producing foods you ate. Some babies are sensitive to caffeine as well. If you think certain foods may be causing your breastfeeding baby to be fussy, then avoid those foods for several days and see if you notice any difference.

Remember, no one knows your baby as you do, and if you sense that something is wrong physically, do not hesitate to call the pediatrician.

Need to Suck on Something. Many babies find it comforting or soothing to suck on something, whether it is a clean finger or a pacifier. First, make sure that your baby is not hungry since newborns most often need to have their sucking instinct satisfied with the nutrition of breastmilk or formula, rather than the nonnutritive sucking of a pacifier. Once you have ensured that the baby is not hungry, then offer him a pacifier, teething ring, or a clean finger to suck on until he calms down.

Time of Day. Sometimes there are simply times of the day that a baby may become fussy. One of my daughters typically had a crying spell in the early evening, which made dinner preparation a tad bit of a challenge, yet this routine only lasted a short while.

Creative Ways to Console

There's no one perfect solution to console a crying baby, but there are a few creative ideas moms have used throughout the years to help soothe the tears. Try several of these methods to see which ones may work for your precious one.

Rocking. As anyone who has ever whiled away the hours on a porch swing knows, there is something calming about a gentle rocking motion. Consider standing with your baby in your arms and swaying back and forth, rocking in a rocking chair or glider, or placing the baby in a baby swing.

Change of Venue. Putting your baby in the stroller and taking him for a walk may be calming for both you and him. Another helpful idea is to put your baby in the car seat and take him for a ride. Perhaps a quiet, dark room or a different setting is all he needs to regain some composure.

A Snug Wrap. A swaddling wrap is a way of firmly wrapping a newborn, helping him feel more secure. Here's one way to swaddle your baby: Spread a receiving or lightweight blanket on the floor. Fold one corner of the blanket down. Lay baby faceup on the blanket with his head just above the folded end. Pick up either the right or left side of the blanket and pull it over your baby to tuck it in snugly under his opposite side. Fold up the bottom of the blanket to cover his feet, then wrap the remaining side of the blanket around him, keeping his head and neck exposed. Do not wrap too tightly, and do not leave your baby in a swaddle wrap for more than eight hours in a row. I recommend a blanket called the Miracle Blanket, which is created especially for babies as a swaddling wrap.[3]

Singing or Consistent Rhythm. Your baby was accustomed to the rhythm of your heartbeat while in the womb, and some newborns are soothed by a similarly consistent rhythm. Consider gently humming or singing a lullaby to soothe your fussy baby. I sang "Jesus Loves Me" and other simple Bible songs to calm my babies. Some parents have found that the rhythm of the washing machine or dishwasher can help.

Pacifier or Teething Ring. Some babies have a strong desire or natural reflex to suck. A pacifier may be the calming factor your child needs. Usually between three to eight months old, babies begin cutting teeth, which may increase irritability. Excessive drooling, biting, or even a mild temperature may be an indication that a tooth is surfacing. To soothe your baby's gums, offer him a cold, wet washcloth, a refrigerated (not frozen) teething ring, or teething biscuits.

Baby Massage. Gently rub or massage your baby's back or tummy to help soothe the crying.

Stimulation. Although one reason babies cry is from overstimulation, it can also be possible that your baby is bored and may need attention or stimuli. There are plenty of baby boredom busters on the market. Visit your local toy store or do a search for "smart baby toys" on the Web.

Gas Remedies. It is possible that your baby may need to be burped or needs to be fed in a more upright position to avoid gas pains. If your baby arches his back or draws up his knees in pain, he is likely to be suffering from gas. You may want to consider Mylicon Infant Gas Relief, which is safe for newborns and available over the counter at most pharmacies. Sometimes babies have an intolerance or allergy to certain foods. A simple change in diet may make a difference.

> It is important for you to try to stay as calm as possible if your baby is colicky.

Colic. Mayo Clinic estimates that 5 to 25 percent of babies have a frustrating period of inconsolable and intense crying known as colic.[4] Colic is typically defined as crying for more than three hours a day, three days a week, for more than three weeks in an otherwise well-fed, healthy baby. Generally the episodes show up in the late afternoon or evening. A colicky baby may be difficult or even impossible to console during these crying episodes.

In addition to trying the methods already mentioned in this chapter, it is important for you to try to stay as calm as possible if your baby is colicky. I know it is difficult to remain relaxed in the midst of incessant crying, but your baby can pick up on your stress and tension. Again, don't hesitate to ask—call a friend or see if your spouse can give you just a short break. Use the opportunity to take a quick nap, read, talk to another adult, take a shower, or simply step out of the house in order to regain your composure. If there is no one to call at the time, then you may need to lay your baby safely in his crib and step into another room for a while.

Take Care of Yourself. It can be unnerving to hear your baby constantly cry. If you have gone through the checklist of possible reasons your baby is crying and nothing seems to fit, then take a few measures so that you do not become overwhelmed. Sometimes, you may need to put your baby down and let him cry for a while, or you can put on some relaxing music to calm your spirit and help you not focus on the cries.

How to Tell If You Are Depressed

If you are experiencing signs of postpartum depression, please do not be hard on yourself. Physically you are feeling blue and perhaps can't make the choice to see things in a positive way.

The National Women's Health Information Center provides the following symptoms of depression. Any of these symptoms during and after pregnancy that last longer than two weeks are signs of postpartum depression:

- Feeling restless or irritable
- Feeling sad, hopeless, and overwhelmed
- Crying a lot
- Having no energy or motivation

- Eating too little or too much
- Sleeping too little or too much
- Trouble focusing, remembering, or making decisions
- Feeling worthless and guilty
- Loss of interest or pleasure in activities
- Withdrawal from friends and family
- Having headaches, chest pains, heart palpitations (heart beating fast and feeling like it is skipping beats), or hyperventilation (fast and shallow breathing)
- Being afraid of hurting the baby or oneself or not having any interest in the baby.

If you recognize that you need help, please contact a physician today. Do not put it off. You may need some medication to get you through this period of time when hormones are affecting your ability to cope.

In addition to seeking proper medical treatment for your depression, try some of the following options, recommended by the National Women's Health Information Center:

- Talk to someone who will listen (friend, relative, or spouse).
- Try to get as much rest as you can.
- Stop putting pressure on yourself to do everything—ask for help.
- Don't spend a lot of time alone.
- Get dressed and leave the house to run an errand or take a short walk.
- Talk with other mothers so you can learn from their experiences.[5]

For Crying Out Loud

There will probably be times when you feel as if you are absolutely going to fall apart or lose your mind if your baby doesn't stop crying! If you feel this way, you are not alone. Consider calling a friend or relative for support, encouragement, and help. Please don't feel like a failure if you need to call someone to come over and give you an hour's relief if you think you are going to explode. Do an online search or look in your local yellow pages to find a local moms group for support.

Please try to remember that this phase won't last forever. Your baby will eventually stop crying, although you cannot see the end right now. And remember, no matter how frustrated or angry you are with your baby's crying, never, ever resort to the physical means of shaking or hitting your baby to express your frustration.

> These frazzled times are trying to a mom's soul, yet they can also be a time of maturity and growth.

These frazzled times are trying to a mom's soul, yet they can also be a time of maturity and growth. It's a stretching time of personal growth in the areas of selflessness, patience, perseverance, and love. Personal growth is rarely easy; it comes with a cost. As the mom of a new baby, you may not have too many quiet moments to yourself. You are learning to serve for more hours with less sleep, and it is difficult.

Are you up for the challenge? You can choose to grumble and live in constant frustration, or you can choose to see this as a growth time and cry out to God for strength.

Motherhood is not an easy role, and a crying baby can be one of the most frustrating parts of the job. Dear fellow mom, this may be one of the most stretching times in your life, yet it is one of the most glorious times as well because God is developing in you a beautiful servant's heart. Jesus said if we want to be great in God's kingdom, we must learn to be servants of all. Thank You, Lord, for teaching us such a valuable and eternal lesson through our precious babies.

Love Notes from God

*I cry out to the L*ORD*;*
  *I plead for the L*ORD*'s mercy.*
I pour out my complaints before him
  and tell him all my troubles.
For I am overwhelmed,
and you alone know the way I should turn.
Wherever I go,
  my enemies have set traps for me.
I look for someone to come and help me,
  but no one gives me a passing thought!
No one will help me;
  no one cares a bit what happens to me.
*Then I pray to you, O L*ORD*.*
  I say, "You are my place of refuge.
  You are all I really want in life.
Hear my cry,
  for I am very low.
Rescue me from my persecutors,
  for they are too strong for me.
 Bring me out of prison
  so I can thank you.
The godly will crowd around me,
  for you treat me kindly." (Ps. 142:1–7 NLT*)*

The righteous cry out, and the LORD hears,
And delivers them out of all their troubles.
The LORD is near to those who have a broken heart,
And saves such as have a contrite spirit. (Ps. 34:17–18 NKJV)

Even as adults we need to cry sometimes. We can always cry out to our heavenly Father. Just think: the God of all creation bends His ears to hear our cries! So in your deepest despair, remember to cry out to God, who loves you.

God is sufficient to meet our needs. Are you tired? Cry out to Him for strength. Are you overwhelmed? Cry to the One who can calm your spirit. God is able to give you whatever you need for the moment. He loves you and wants you to cry out to Him.

■ ■ ■

How does it help me to know that God hears my cry?

8

Triumph Over Toddler Tantrums

Now may the God of patience and comfort grant you to be
like-minded toward one another, according to Christ Jesus.
—ROMANS 15:5 NKJV

Even though children are deductible,
they can also be very taxing.
—FROM *Nelson's Big Book of Laughter*[1]

young father pushed the grocery cart through the store as his two-year-old son screamed in a full-blown tantrum. A nearby mother heard the dad saying in a very controlled tone, "Stay calm, Kevin. You can do this, Kevin. It will be okay, Kevin. You can make it through, Kevy Boy; just a few more aisles to go."

The mom was impressed with the father's calm response. She said, "Sir, I must commend you on the kind way you are trying to console your son Kevin."

With a sheepish look, the man admitted, "Lady, I'm Kevin!"

Oh, the joys of toddler tantrums in public places! How many times have you been humbled in the last few years? The time I abandoned a cart full of groceries (representing an hour's worth of shopping carefully with coupons) in utter humiliation due to a crying baby and a toddler meltdown stands out in my memory. Even the most well-mannered, even-tempered child will have a temper tantrum now and then. These behavior blowouts usually occur in children between the ages of one to three. Wouldn't it be lovely if these fits only happened infrequently at home? Unfortunately, they are more apt to take place in public or at the in-laws'.

If only it were other people's children who experienced temper tantrums, not our sweet angels! Yet temper tantrums are a normal part of development as children work through their frustrations and independence. Although the information in this chapter cannot eradicate every toddler tantrum, it can help you prevent some tantrums and give you tools to handle them when they do erupt.

As moms, we want to do all we can to defuse our toddlers' tempers and help our children gain more self-control.

Why Toddlers' Tempers Flare

What makes our calm and charming children turn into red-faced, screaming, kicking monsters? We can't know exactly what is ticking in their little brains, but we can decode some of their messages. It is important for us moms to understand the potential reasons our children throw fits, so we can prevent the tantrums if possible or deal with them appropriately.

Tantrums often occur when a child is hungry, tired, frustrated, bored, overstimulated, or seeking attention. A tantrum can be the result of a child not being able to do a task or not getting what he wants. Also, a child can become overwhelmed and frustrated when he doesn't have the capability to do a specific task quite yet.

In these early years, a child's language is developing, and he tends to understand more than he can express. Toddlers experience extreme frustration when they are unable to communicate what they want. Think if you were staying in a hotel in a foreign country and you needed to order room service. Imagine the frustration of trying to get exactly what you want when you can only speak one or two words of the language. Now you may not throw a temper tantrum (at least I hope not!), but children don't have the inhibitions we have as adults. They haven't learned through years of maturity how to stay calm when they are frustrated (okay, so we haven't learned it so well ourselves as adults). The good news is as a child's language skills develop and he learns self-control, these tantrums often dissipate.

Toddlers are also growing in their need for autonomy. They begin to develop a sense of independence and desire more control over their situations or environments. Unfortunately, they are not quite capable of handling such independence, and this can create a power struggle and/or an angry outburst. They want to be able to do a task by themselves or have it their way. Learning to do tasks with confidence is not a bad thing, but we must gently help our toddlers until they are ready to handle tasks on their own. When they demand their way or cry for something they want but can't have, this becomes a learning time as well. Possibly one of the most important lessons we can teach our kids is that we don't get everything we want and we don't always get our way. The lesson begins in these important early years.

> Possibly one of the most important lessons we can teach our kids is that we don't get everything we want and we don't always get our way.

When we step back and look at the reasons toddlers throw fits, they generally fall into two categories: frustration or manipulation. Frustration outbursts are due to an inability to communicate or being tired or hungry, and they should be handled differently than a manipulative tantrum from a child who is trying to get his mommy to buy him a baseball or coloring book.

Let's take a look at how to handle tantrums while keeping both motivations in mind.

Handling the Tantrum

No matter what the reason for the outburst of rage, the first and most important rule for moms is to stay calm. If you allow yourself to become angry and out of control, then you have two tantrums on your hands—and that's not a pretty sight. Besides, if you scream and yell, you teach your child two lessons: you can get someone's attention through screaming, and it is okay to scream because Mommy does it. So, rule number one in handling your child's tantrum is to keep your cool and speak to your child in calm and soothing tones.

You need to be the strong one, but if you are at your wit's end, keep in mind the STOP method we learned in Chapter 5: **S**tep away, **T**ake several deep breaths, **O**bjectively look at the situation, and **P**ray. Seek God's help, patience, and discernment about how to help your child. Remember, don't take your toddler's tantrum personally. Your child is not doing this to embarrass you. He is doing this because he is frustrated and can't communicate, or he urgently wants something. If you remain calm, you are better able to think clearly and try to understand what is going on with your child.

Try the following methods to handle the tantrum. Not all of them will work with your toddler, but explore and begin to figure out which ones are effective for calming down your child.

Verbalize the Frustration. Gently help your child verbalize his frustration or say it for him. "Mommy knows you are mad because you can't buckle the car seat by yourself. Let's do it together." Do not try to negotiate with your child; simply let him know you understand what he is trying to do or have.

Hold Your Child. Sometimes when a child has lost control, he needs a secure and loving embrace to help him calm down. Some kids do not respond well to being held. One of my daughters liked to be held during a tantrum, but the other didn't; she became more enraged as she tried to get away. Know your child. Boys especially may need to be released to work out their frustration physically.

Move Your Child to Another Location. If you have a childproofed room or a fenced-in yard where your child can work out his tantrum, remove him from the source of frustration and allow him to work it through by himself. Remain in fairly close proximity so he knows you haven't left him, but don't give attention to the tantrum. If you are in a public place, you may want to take him outside or to the bathroom in order to change the environment.

Firmly and Gently Tell Your Child No. If you know your child's tantrum is manipulative, then lovingly and firmly explain that you are not going to give him what he wants. Stick with your firm no. Tell him when he calms down you will work out a solution or alternative. If you are at home, let him cry it out—he will eventually stop. If you are in a public place, you may need to move him to another room or outside until he gains composure and sees that you mean no.

Recently, I observed a mother and toddler in the seats in front of me on a plane. When the boy began to scream and cry because he wanted the trailer that went with his toy truck, the mom gently took his face and said in a soft, firm voice, "No, we don't scream on the plane." The boy calmed down. Then this wise mom offered him hope. "Perhaps Grandma or Uncle Bill has a trailer you can put on your truck." The boy was content, for his mother affirmed that she heard him, let him know what was expected of him, and then she offered hope.

Offer Hope. We all need a glimmer of hope. Whenever you tell your child no, if possible, offer hope for something different down the road.

With no hope in sight, a child can become discouraged or exasperated, but if you provide him alternatives and possibilities, he may be calmed and encouraged.

Distract Your Child. This is a useful tool if you know the tantrum is born out of frustration. Toddlers have short attention spans, so a distraction can take their minds off the immediate source of tension. If you are at the store, ask your child to help you find the next purchase, or look for something that is his favorite color. If you are at home, distract him with a new project or different toy. On occasion a child may be bored and need something to keep him stimulated. Bring extra toys or snacks whenever you leave the house.

Ignore the Tantrum. If you are at home and you can tell the tantrum leans more toward manipulation, then do your best to ignore the tantrum. You may want to move to another room—but if your child is young, don't leave her sight as she may feel very insecure. If you are in a public place, then ignoring the tantrum may not be the best solution, but you can move your child to a different place.

Do Not Allow Aggressive Behavior. Don't ignore a tantrum if your child becomes violent with you or someone else. At this point, it is time for disciplinary action as he must learn to curb this behavior. Tell your child you will not allow him to hurt others, remove him from the situation, and then punish him accordingly.

Shopping with Tired Toddlers and Other Scary Scenarios

Never underestimate the power of prevention. Through wisdom and discernment, we can help our children avoid potential angry fits. Certainly we can't prevent all of our kids' tantrums, but we can move around many potential land mines so we have fewer explosions. Here are a few toddler land mines to avoid as moms.

Terrible Timing. Don't run errands when the kids are tired, hungry, or overstimulated. Make a general plan for your day, and if at all possible, run errands in the morning while the kids are more alert and energetic. Be careful not to overdo it. Attempting too many errands in one day is a tantrum waiting to happen. Avoid long outings whenever possible, and make sure you allow time for food and opportunities for your child to get out of the stroller or car seat to stretch his legs and run off some energy.

Lack of Preparation. You know your child. If she needs extra snacks, bring them along. If she often gets thirsty, bring extra juice or water. If your child can't stand wet or soiled clothes, bring a change of clothing, and always make sure you have enough diapers on hand. Another important preventative measure is to bring some toys and books for those times when you find yourself unexpectedly waiting in traffic, in a restaurant, or in the grocery store line.

Inconsistency. No means no. Unless some sort of extenuating circumstance occurs, you must stick to your guns. If you give in to a tantrum, your child will learn that screaming works. Be gentle and firm, but don't change your mind just to quiet your child down. Use a creative distraction or alternative if you must.

Too Many Rules. We set ourselves up for sabotage if we create too many rules in our homes. Keep your rules simple and easy to obey so it is not necessary to say no every time you turn around. You only frustrate a child with too many nos. Be reasonable and open. Toddler-proof your house for the time being so every other word coming out of your mouth is not a rule or reprimand.

Lack of Attention. Kids need, desire, and even thrive on quality time with you. Make sure you take time each day for some good old eye-to-eye communication with your child. Sometimes we get so busy doing activities and interests for our children (or for ourselves) that we forget to give them very essential undivided attention. I'm not saying you need to overattend your child (which some moms are in danger of), but I am saying just as you feed your child each day, be sure to feed him the delicious gift of your attention as well.

No Choices. As your child's independent spirit develops, give him opportunities to make simple decisions. "Do you want to read this book or that one?" "Do you want the orange sippy cup or the pink one?"

> Make sure you take time each day for some good old eye-to-eye communication with your child.

Non-Age-Appropriate Activities. Let's not give our kids a ticket to frustration by placing them in activities or giving them tasks that are over their heads. Teach and stretch, yes. But there is a delicate balance between teaching and expecting too much. If you give your children age-appropriate toys and provide age-appropriate activities, you set the stage for success rather than frustration.

Uncommunicated Expectations. Always remember to tell your child how you expect him to act, especially as you approach a new situation. On the way to the playground, say, "Honey, I expect you to obey Mommy. We will eat lunch and play, but then we must leave when I say so for little Kelsey's naptime."

Failure to Commend Good Behavior. Take advantage of the times your kids do something right, and tell them, "Good job! I'm proud of you." Kids love attention and encouragement and will strive to live up to the kind words you say about them. You can bet if you tell your child, "I'm so proud of you for not being fussy at the grocery store today," he will work hard not to whine or complain the next time you go.

Junk food. Sugar, caffeine, and junk foods affect the body's ability to handle stress. Feed your children wholesome foods that will sustain them longer and give them strength to adjust and persevere, instead of becoming hyper. You may detect that your child is wild after eating certain types of foods. If so, begin eliminating different foods from your child's diet and see if his behavior is affected. I discovered orange juice tended to make my older daughter a little out of sorts, so we removed it from her diet.

Overstimulation. Too many activities, too many people, and too much sugar can be a recipe for disaster. Guard against overstimulation by recognizing the needs of your child. Some kids thrive in a busy or loud environment while others explode from sensory overload. Turn off the television or music and move into a peaceful room with fewer people when you begin to see the first stages of overstimulated fussiness.

Lone Ranger Parenting. Build a team with those who spend the most time with your kids. Explain to your spouse, the grandparents, or a favorite sitter how you plan to handle tantrums and how to prevent them. Ask them to join you in the effort. The more consistent the main players are in your kids' lives, the quicker your children will learn that tantrums get them nowhere.

And that's the goal to keep in mind: you are gently trying to teach your children that tantrums are not a healthy way to get what they want. Tantrums are not a becoming quality for an adult, so we need to help our children get rid of tantrums as they begin to grow up and leave the toddler years behind.

Important Life Lessons

Instead of dreading the tantrum years, let's look at them as a tremendous opportunity to teach our children some of life's most important lessons. Yes, the toddler years are often a struggle, but they are also a time of growth and laying a foundation for our children's futures.

Here are a few life lessons our children can learn through the process of working through their toddler fits:

- I can't have everything I want.
- I don't get to do everything I want to do.
- Change happens, and I must be flexible.
- Mistakes happen, and I must forgive and move on.
- I am not capable of doing everything on my own. I sometimes need the help of others.
- Respect and self-control work. Screaming and whining don't.

If our kids can toddle away from these early years having learned these lessons, then we have helped them down the road to success.

Keep these life lessons in the forefront of your mind as the goal you are working toward. The list will give you encouragement and strength and remind you that good will come from this difficult stage as you handle your child's tantrums with wisdom.

I wish I could tell you these lessons are sealed in stone once our kids emerge for the tantrum stage victoriously, but I must warn you these same lessons may resurface during the adolescent years. Look at each of these opportunities as a positive time of growth, instead of a time of fear and dread for the parents. All in all, these years are filled with precious times of joy and wonder, with a few rough spots of growing and learning mixed in each day.

Love Notes from God

When Israel was a child, I loved him as a son, and I called my son out of Egypt. But the more I called to him, the more he rebelled, offering

*sacrifices to the images of Baal and burning incense to idols. It was I
who taught Israel how to walk, leading him along by the hand. But he
doesn't know or even care that it was I who took care of him. I led Israel
along with my ropes of kindness and love. I lifted the yoke from his
neck, and I myself stooped to feed him.* (Hos. 11:1–4 NLT)

*I will heal their backsliding,
I will love them freely,
For My anger has turned away from him.
I will be like the dew to Israel;
He shall grow like the lily,
And lengthen his roots like Lebanon.
His branches shall spread;
His beauty shall be like an olive tree,
And his fragrance like Lebanon.* (Hos. 14:4–6 NKJV)

Through the prophet Hosea, the Lord reassures Israel of His
redeeming, abiding, fatherly love for them. God Himself knows
the joys and the challenges of parenting the young nation of
Israel (like a young child), as He describes in the passage above.

Dear fellow mom, take comfort in going to Him with
your needs and concerns. He knows your challenges and is
able to give you the strength, patience, and wisdom to make
it through these early years. He is able to make these years
fruitful and significant in your child's life.

■ ■ ■

*How does God care for my daily needs as His precious young
child?*

9

Understanding Your Child

Discipline your children,
and they will give you happiness and peace of mind.
—PROVERBS 29:17 NLT

Children need love,
especially when they do not deserve it.
—HAROLD S. HULBERT

How precious and innocent is the heart of a child! Kids see the world in simplicity and truth. Generally speaking, their worldview has not yet been jaded or tarnished by evil people or intentional harm. They haven't had the time, capacity, or opportunity to become bitter or cynical. No wonder Jesus said, "Let the little children come to Me, and do not forbid them; for of such is the kingdom of heaven" (Matt. 19:14 NKJV). These early years offer parents the wonderful opportunity to instill in their children a love and respect for God and for people.

When our kids are between the ages of four and nine, we begin to learn and understand a little more about them and appreciate who they are as individual creations of God. Since our children are now able to verbalize and express their thoughts and emotions, we are invited to know them on a deeper level. We begin to see their gifts, talents, personality traits, and abilities emerge, and we can encourage them in the right direction. We also begin to see some of their fears and weaknesses surface as well.

Possibly one of the most important truths we must grasp as parents during these younger years is the fact that our children are still children. They are "works in progress," developing and growing in their own personal skills. They are also learning trust, obedience, respect, self-control, kindness, patience, and attentiveness. They are not graduates of these fine lessons yet. Our job as parents is to patiently teach and train and help our children develop, and not to belittle them because they "just don't get it." You and I are still growing and learning as well. Aren't you glad that God doesn't stand there in heaven, wagging His finger at us in frustration and saying, "When are you finally going to learn?"

We must lead, help, discipline, and guide our young children. During this stage of growth, I also encourage you to set the stage for helping your children grow in love and faith in God. This is a significant time for our kids to begin to learn about the sovereign God who loves them and has a plan for their lives.

Your Unique Child

What a privilege and a joy it is for parents to unwrap the beautiful gifts God has given us in our children! No two kids are exactly the same. Even identical twins have unique gifts and personalities. It is important to let our children know we recognize them as unique creations of God. They each give and receive love a bit differently. Each child expresses anger differently than the rest of his family members. Appreciate the uniqueness of your child instead of expecting him to be just like everyone else.

Our job as moms is to partner with the Lord and join Him in what He is doing in our children's lives. Join with me in prayer:

Wonderful Creator, loving heavenly Father, You know my child better than I will ever know him. You know his heart and his mind, and You have gifted him with certain abilities and talents. He also has weaknesses of which You are well aware. Most importantly, You have a plan and a purpose for him. Oh Lord, use me to help encourage his gifts and talents and set him in the right direction. Pour Your love through me so together we may build on his strengths and work around his weaknesses. Work out Your perfect will for him, and please use me as a positive influence in the process. In Jesus' name, amen.

As we pray for our kids and for our work as moms, we entrust God to do a greater work than we can do ourselves. Let's decide right now to give our cares and worries about our kids' futures over to God. Instead of fretting, let's give God our concerns and seek His direction and wisdom every day. He loves our kids and knows them better than we know them. May we see our role as joining together with God to encourage the best in our kids.

How to Respond to Our Kids' Anger

In *How to Really Parent Your Child,* Dr. Ross Campbell states, "Training in anger management is the most crucial and difficult task that faces you as a parent. If you can successfully point the way toward healthy handling of anger, your child will be able to resolve most other problems as well; if not, nearly everything in life will be damaged by a rampant spirit of rage."[1]

When our kids outwardly express their anger, our response may be to squelch it right away because it may be loud or embarrassing or destructive. Instead of denying that the anger is there, the more important approach is to help our children recognize their anger and teach them to deal with it in an appropriate manner. As we teach our kids to handle their anger in a positive way during these early years, we point them toward the pathway for successful social interaction in the years to come. The following three-step plan is designed to help you teach your children how to handle their anger.

> **Our kids learn the loudest lessons from our own behavior.**

Step One: Model a Healthy Expression of Anger. We cannot ignore that the most important way to teach our kids how to handle their anger is to be good models ourselves. Our kids learn the loudest lessons from our own behavior. If they see us continually yelling and demeaning them or other people, they will assume that behavior is effective and acceptable. Our role begins with our own expressions of anger. Periodically ask yourself, "Am I modeling a healthy and positive way to deal with anger?" With each new stage in our children's lives, we must adjust to handling their anger in new and fresh ways, so we must return to this question often. Please also return to Chapter 3 in order to refresh yourself on healthy ways to handle your own anger.

Step Two: Help Your Kids Recognize Their Angry Feelings. Children can become frustrated and irritated for a number of reasons. It could be a conflict over possessions. It may be an unkind remark or a shove from another child. Young ones may get angry over not getting their way or not having what they want. It may be they don't want to comply or obey, so they become upset and emotional. Whatever the reason, it is important for them to identify their anger, so they can deal with it properly.

As parents, we can help our kids label what they are feeling:

- You seem mad.
- Are you irritated?
- What seems to be frustrating you?
- How are you feeling right now?

A visual picture can help kids understand the levels of anger. Create a "Get a Grip on Anger" poster to help them learn the different levels of anger. On the poster, draw a line across the middle. At one end of the line write "A Little Mad," and on the other end of the line write "Boiling Over." Together, think of where words like the following should be placed on the line: *irritated, frustrated, very mad, fuming, rattled,* and *furious.* For young ones, plot the words yourself and even draw pictures to help define the feelings. This will help your kids identify the different levels of anger everyone experiences and will give them a reference point for times when they are angry.

Sometimes kids experience early warning signs when they are feeling angry or frustrated. Talk with your children about some of the signs they may have, such as clenching fists, pounding heart rate, faster breathing, breaking out in a sweat, or talking louder. As they begin identifying the early warning signs as well as labeling some of the early feelings of anger, they can begin to employ self-control and other healthy ways to handle their frustrations. Anger can escalate quickly, so it is important to recognize it early before it gets out of control.

Step Three: Help Your Kids Express Their Anger in a Positive Way. Help your kids think of ways they can calm down when they feel angry. You may want to add a few suggestions to the bottom or back of your Get a Grip on Anger poster. Consider actions such as gently discussing the issue with the person, walking away from the situation that is making you angry, or choosing to do something else. You may also suggest distractions as ways to work out angry feelings, such as run around the block, jump on the trampoline, climb a tree, scream into a pillow, play on the swing set, shoot hoops, draw a picture, build something, talk to someone about the situation. If you live near a pond or creek, consider skipping stones in the water.

Music can have a calming effect, so perhaps your child could choose to listen to some of his favorite music or play an instrument to help him settle down. Harp music worked for King Saul in the Bible. You may have something constructive your child can do, such as help bring in firewood or help fold laundry, not as a punishment but rather as a way to do something helpful and constructive, getting his mind off the anger. Boys may have different ways of responding to anger from girls, so it is important to allow each child to identify his or her own "best" ways to work out anger.

Consider teaching your children a simple version of the STOP method described in Chapter 5. As they feel the early warning signs of anger, teach them to Step away from the situation or person that is making them upset. Then remind them to Take several deep, soothing breaths to calm down physically. Practice together taking at least three deep, slow breaths from their tummy area. Tell them to take a moment to Objectively look at the situation—and consider positive ways to handle their anger. Then encourage your children to Pray and seek God's help in maintaining self-control.

We must also help our children to learn what it means to overlook an affront or forgive another person. We can teach our kids, even at an early age, that forgiveness is a gift we give to others. It is beautiful how easily kids can forgive one another. What happened to us adults? Teaching kids the importance of boundaries is another valuable lesson so they don't continue to be hurt. We can begin teaching them to confront certain issues or hurts and, if necessary, go to the person who offended them. We'll discuss the issue of forgiveness in more depth in Chapter 14.

Consequences of Mismanagement

It is our role to teach our kids that there are consequences if they choose to handle their anger in a destructive way. You may want to mention a few destructive ways people may handle anger (hitting, saying bad words, screaming, getting revenge, and so on). Teach your kids when they are young that these are inappropriate and ineffective ways to handle anger. Your children need to learn that if they choose to handle their anger in a negative fashion rather than a positive one, there will be consequences. You and your husband can decide on an effective punishment ahead of time and tell your children what it will be. Making these decisions outside of the heat of the moment is much more constructive and allows you to be more consistent.

In order for a punishment to be effective, it must be painful. You know your child and what will be painful to him. One child may value a certain television show while another may love having friends over or going to a friend's house, so taking away these privileges may be effective. Other children may find it painful to do a chore or write a note of apology. You know your child and the type of correction that will speak to him. Be pragmatic. If one punishment does not seem to curb a negative behavior, then consider a new one.

Moving in the Right Direction

Remember, these are learning years. Don't become frustrated if your child doesn't begin handling his or her anger correctly right away.

We're still learning, aren't we? Be gentle and patient. You are training your children and helping them to form positive habits. Learning to manage anger doesn't happen overnight; rather, it happens through a period of stumbles and falls and getting back up and trying again. Lead by example, train in gentleness, and discipline in love.

You can make a powerful and lasting impact on your kids by patiently training them now. Their friends, teachers, and future spouses will thank you for staying the course and being steadfast in your goal to teach your kids about wise anger management. We don't want our kids to stuff or hide or ignore their anger, for we know it will eventually come out in an explosion of some sort. We do want to teach our kids to recognize their angry feelings and learn self-control through anger management and forgiveness.

> *Persistent* and *consistent* are the two key words for us as moms.

Persistent and *consistent* are the two key words for us as moms. Persistence reminds us not to give up or throw in the towel. We need the reminder to be persistent as we continue to model positive ways to handle our anger and teach our kids how to do the same. We will eventually see results. Consistency is key in training your child in the way he should go. As you apply gentle persistence in teaching and a wise consistency in discipline, you will see a thoughtful and mature youth emerge.

Love Notes from God

Love suffers long and is kind; love does not envy; love does not parade itself, is not puffed up; does not behave rudely, does not seek its own, is not provoked, thinks no evil; does not rejoice in iniquity, but rejoices in the truth; bears all things, believes all things, hopes all things, endures all things. Love never fails. But whether there are prophecies, they will fail; whether there are tongues, they will cease; whether there is knowledge, it will vanish away. For we know in part and we prophesy in part. But when that which is perfect has come, then that which is in part will be done away.

When I was a child, I spoke as a child, I understood as a child, I thought as a child; but when I became a man, I put away childish things. For now we see in a mirror, dimly, but then face to face. Now I know in part, but then I shall know just as I also am known.

And now abide faith, hope, love, these three; but the greatest of these is love. (1 Cor. 13:4–13 NKJV)

We all fall far short of sincerely, graciously loving others. The love described in 1 Corinthians 13 is not a natural human love, but it is a picture of God's pure love. Oh, if we only realized that we are loved by our heavenly Father with so great, so pure, so beautiful a love! May we receive His love and allow it to pour through us and overflow from us to others.

In this passage, we also see an analogy to a child. Our concept and understanding of God is like that of a child right now. We may not understand all God's ways and why He allows certain things in our lives, but we can trust His great love for us. It makes you think of your own children, doesn't it?

■ ■ ■

In what ways am I childlike in my understanding of God's ways?

How does knowing this help me relate to my kids?

10

Riding the Storms of Adolescent Hormones

And God is able to make all grace abound toward you,
that you, always having all sufficiency in all things,
may have an abundance for every good work.
—2 CORINTHIANS 9:8 NKJV

Adolescence is like a house on moving day—
a temporary mess.
—JULIUS E. WARREN

*Y*ou thought you knew your child. He was a respectful and caring young person. Life was going along on a fairly smooth road. All of the sudden, out of the blue, your nice, calm drive down Parenthood Lane was shaken by an enormously unpredictable rocky patch, full of potholes. Welcome to Adolescent Avenue, a place where emerging hormones begin to rock your family's world. Sorry to say, there is no detour around this rocky road, but through wise strategies and discerning shock absorbers, we can navigate through these years without too many bumps along the way.

Please don't dread these years. There can be such joy during this time. Often we only hear the bad side of adolescence, but it is important for parents to recognize the good points of these years as well.

Teenagers can be thoughtful, energetic, concerned about right and wrong, and feel things deeply. They tend to be idealistic and emotionally sensitive. Our goal as parents of teenagers should be to help nurture their good qualities and help them develop their gifts and talents, and also to help them steer away from negative behaviors.

The adolescent years are an essential time for us to reassure our kids of our unconditional love for them. We need to build their confidence, helping them understand some of the physical and emotional changes they are going through. Remember, an adolescent child is on a rocky road, too, sometimes not understanding why he acts the way he does. As we recognize what is going on inside our kids, we are better able to respond to their behavior.

Road Map to Understanding

Confusion! Fear! Dread! Everything is larger than life!

Am I describing the latest horror movie? No, it's adolescence. I wouldn't want to relive those years if you paid me; would you? Every young person must go through this period of struggle and growth along the path to independence.

Each child handles the adolescent years a little differently. Early adolescence occurs around ages ten to fifteen, but some girls may show signs as early as eight years old. This is a time of change in our kids' lives as they begin to develop patterns of thinking and behaving that may be with them for years—even into adulthood. They begin to think more abstractly and start forming personal moral codes.

"Many kids announce the onset of adolescence with a dramatic change in behavior around their parents. They're starting to separate from Mom and Dad and to become more independent," says Dr. Barbara P. Homeier. "At the same time, kids this age are increasingly aware of how others, especially their peers, see them and they're desperately trying to fit in."[1]

At times your teenager may feel his or her mind, body, or mouth is out of control. A young teen may experience a surge of anger over a seemingly simple suggestion or request. Often teenagers act in ways they didn't intend to act or say things in the heat of the moment that they didn't mean to say. Feelings of self-doubt and inferiority reach an all-time high, and they care immensely about what their peers think.

Dr. James Dobson tells parents, "An adolescent's sense of worth as a human being hangs precariously on peer-group acceptance, which can be tough to garner. Thus, relatively minor evidences of rejection or ridicule are of major significance to those who already see themselves as fools and failures."[2]

Pillow or Punishment

Teenagers' anger and frustration may stem from a wide range of internal or external struggles. They may be acting out their hurt over not having anyone to sit with at lunch, or they may be frustrated about their performance at football practice, or perhaps they are upset from the embarrassment of being ridiculed by a classmate. Their angry outbursts toward you may not be a result of disobedience, and they may not intend to be disrespectful. Often they are hurting and need to be reassured they are loved unconditionally. As parents, we must be a "pillow" to our teenagers. Our cushioned response to their prickly surface will help them through these difficult years much more than a harsh, angry reaction.

It is certainly human for us to react unfavorably when someone is angry or frustrated, especially if it seems as if his emotions are directed toward us. Our natural desire is to set our children straight, cap off their anger, and fix their problems. What we really need to do is respond gently and allow them to work through their anger in a positive way, and discipline if necessary. Don't try to deny their feelings or tell them they shouldn't feel that way; instead, recognize they feel the way they do and listen to them and try to point them in a new direction. There are times when teenagers do something embarrassing or make a mistake, and they think their world will fall apart because of it. They need to be warmly reassured, "Everyone makes mistakes. Forgive yourself and move forward."

> Pointing your teenagers toward something positive helps them work through the pain or frustration they may be feeling.

Your son or daughter may not feel like talking, but some questions may help him or her to open up, such as "Can you tell me something that happened today that is making you feel this way?" or "Tell me one good thing and one awful thing about school today." Gently ask, gently listen, and gently point, with no expectation of how they will respond. That's what being a pillow looks like as a mom.

What do you point them to? Begin with activities or interests your teenagers enjoy or with which they can experience relaxation or some degree of success. Whenever you can put them in a confidence-building situation, do it. Pointing your teenagers toward something positive helps them work through the pain or frustration they may be feeling. Consider some of the following activities:

- Music, playing an instrument or singing
- Journaling, drawing, or painting
- Favorite sports (shoot hoops, throw football or baseball)
- Woodworking, baking, or scrapbooking

- Reading, going to library or bookstore
- Walking, running, hiking, or biking
- Animals (such as horses, pets)
- Rest

Notice I didn't say television, shopping, eating, or video games. We want our kids to find positive, productive outlets for their anger and not form unhealthy habits in dealing with pain or hurts. They will begin feeling better about themselves if they are doing something creative or energizing. The best dose of medicine for both adults and teens is to reach out and help another person, whether it is a friend, a family member, or kids in the local Special Olympics. Now I know those opportunities are not always readily available, but they do offer your teens an opportunity to step outside their own problems and see the bigger world around them. We'll talk more about reaching out in compassion in Chapter 13.

Being a pillow to our kids' emotions doesn't mean we allow them to walk all over us in disrespect. No, it is our responsibility to help them learn and discern the difference between appropriate and inappropriate ways to express anger, and this lesson begins as they learn how to treat us. Being a pillow to our kids means we respond rather than react to their behavior—but when they cross the line of disrespect, we must have clear consequences. Don't be unreasonable, but you and your spouse work together to decide what those lines of respect should be for your family.

You may want to consider household rules of respect, such as: "No degrading or demeaning words to any family member." "No curse words." "No slamming of doors or objects." If your children raise their voices, send them to their rooms until they can return calmly and state their cases in a softer tone. Make sure your rules and discipline are clear so that your kids are not surprised by the punishment. In general, try to keep the rules for your teens to a minimum so you don't have to tell them no all the time and exasperate them in the process.

Recognize right now they are probably not going to respond with a happy attitude to your rules or discipline. As long as your daughter or son is not disrespectful or violent, just let the pouty attitude pass. As pillows, we must choose not to respond to their reactions, knowing that what we are seeing on the surface is really reflecting the turmoil on the inside. Our understanding will help settle them, whereas a rigid and demanding reaction will deepen their lack of confidence and fuel their anger.

Helping Your Teenagers Cope

Trying to help our kids during these rough years may seem futile, yet there are some ways we can extend a hand and help them find their footing as they stumble along. Two starting points are *educate* and *communicate*. Educate yourself about your child, getting to know his situation at school and with friends. Become acquainted with your child's friends and his parents if possible. Invite his friends to your house or offer to drive them to the places they want to go. Often the kids forget you are there, and you can learn a lot about your kids just by listening.

Communicate with your kids as well. Encourage them to tell you how they are feeling or ask for their opinions on certain issues. Talk to them about the consequences of premarital sex, drugs, alcohol, and smoking. Discuss your expectations for them and help them get a sense they are representing both God and your family. Most importantly, communicate often the words, "I love you." Let your teenagers know you love them and think the best of them. Build them up in the areas they are doing right. Send them encouraging e-mails and notes. Talk in a loving manner to your kids and give them words of strength and courage during these unsettling times. Make no mistake: your teenagers feel love through your wise and thoughtful boundaries as well. Certainly, we communicate our love through careful discipline.

> Talk in a loving manner to your kids and give them words of strength and courage during these unsettling times.

Washington Post writer Laura Sessions Stepp spent a year researching the lives of eighteen youths in order to understand what they were going through as adolescents. Her research resulted in the book *Our Last Best Shot, Guiding Our Children Through Early Adolescence.* Stepp shares three significant needs that must be met for adolescents to grow up healthy and strong. The first need is to have a strong identity. Second, they need to have good friends—to be a member of a group and to be a valued member of that group. Third, they need to have opportunities to learn concepts and skills that challenge their growing brain power.

Stepp believes successful parents and teachers consistently demonstrate several similar characteristics: they show respect to children, give them responsibility, and keep relationships going even when kids push away. "You can have all the love in the world for your kid, but if you don't show respect for them, even when they're being disrespectful, they're alienated," Stepp says.[3] In other words, be a pillow during these prickly years. Love and respect your kids through this time. Remember, your kids will learn to respect you and others as they see you model respectful communication.

Our Goals Versus Their Goals

If you were going to write down goals for your children during the teen years, what would you say? Perhaps like me you are thinking, *During these years I would like for my teens to learn and grow into godly, wise, mature young adults.* We also may be secretly thinking, *And I hope they don't rebel, mess up their lives, or embarrass me along the way.* Okay, so now that the truth is out on the table. Honestly, none of us wants our kids to go astray, not only because rebellion can have lifelong consequences for our teens but also because it can make our lives miserable.

Fear often grips parents during these turbulent years. Unfortunately, fear often makes us overreact and set up rule after rule to make sure our kids never step out of line. We tend to worry about inconsequential surface issues, when it is the heart issues we need to be considering. I'm reminded of the conversation James Dobson had with a waitress who recognized him when he walked in for a meal at her restaurant. Business was slow that day, so the waitress began to tell Dr. Dobson about some of the problems she was having with her adolescent daughter. She said she had fought tooth and nail with her daughter for the entire year, and they always fought about the exact same issue. Dr. Dobson asked the waitress what the issue was, and she replied, "My daughter wants to shave her legs. I feel she's too young to be doing that, and she becomes so angry that she won't even talk to me. This has been the worst year of our lives together." Dr. Dobson replied, "Lady, buy your daughter a razor!"[4]

Maybe the issue in your household isn't shaving; maybe it is a messy room or pierced ears or a cell phone. The point is we must be wise and pragmatic as parents and not be so gripped with fear that we fight big battles over little issues. You see, the goal in our teens' hearts is very similar to our goals for them. It comes down to independence. They are growing and learning to make decisions on their own, and they are beginning to break away from having us make every decision for them. Certainly we cannot give them carte blanche to go and do as they please, but we can slowly begin to give them opportunities to make their own wise decisions. Our role is not to parent with rules based on our fears but instead to humbly, prayerfully seek God's wisdom as we make our parenting decisions.

X-Ray Vision Toward Our Teens' Anger

When it comes to brain development, Dr. Campbell says scientists have recently pinpointed a phenomenon that takes place in the teenage brain at the outset of adolescence. "There is an unexpected growth spurt in the frontal cortex, an overproduction of cells just before puberty. It is the first such wave of overproduction since the child was in the womb. The ability to plan, create strategies, and be organized will not come until later. For now, there is a powerful surge of emotional forces but little practical ability to regulate them."

> We must look beyond the surface behavior in our teenagers and recognize that the outward action represents a level of anger or hurt underneath.

Dr. Campbell goes on to say, "This is one of the reasons we have all observed teenagers to be disorganized, sloppy, and ill-planned. Creativity, surging emotions, hormones, and other factors are kicking in—but the brain's 'CEO' or administration resources are simply not ready. So there is a jumble of disorganized emotions. A primary emotion is anger."[5]

We must look beyond the surface behavior in our teenagers and recognize that the outward actions represent a level of anger or hurt underneath. When teens yell at us, slam their books down, roll their eyes, or give loud, rude sighs, our first inclination is to deal with the outward actions perhaps by yelling, "I won't stand for that kind of behavior. Go to your room!" What we often fail to see is there is a world of turmoil underneath the surface that caused the explosion. Certainly we need to teach our kids self-control and ways to handle their expressions of anger appropriately, but we also need to dig deeper. We need to deal not only with the symptoms of anger but also the root of it.

Our kids need to be assured of our unconditional love even when they seem to pull away. We can lovingly help them work through their anger and manage it in a positive way. We want to react, but we must wisely respond. I'm not so good at that—how about you? Day by day as we rely on God's strength and surrender our wills to His, we will begin to reflect His grace as we walk through some of the storms. Sometimes the teen storms form within minutes with no preparation time for us, so we must seek God's face daily to help us in having the self-control we need. Then we can lovingly begin to help our teens learn self-control!

Responding with Love

Wham! You hear the front door slam and loud stomps up the stairs, and you know with abrupt certainty your sixteen-year-old son is home from school. You go upstairs to say a brief "Glad you're home. How was your day?" And all you hear is, "Leave me alone!" as he turns up his music to a wall-shaking decibel level. Your younger daughter yells from her room, "Turn the music down! I'm trying to study!" Then you hear the words that you were hoping wouldn't follow, "Shut up! I'll do what I want!"

Uh-oh. Now you have a choice. You can:

A. Ignore him, pretending you didn't hear him in order to avoid confrontation.
B. Stomp up there, throw open the door, and scream above the music, "What is the matter with you?! You are always in an awful mood and you make our lives miserable!"
C. Stomp up there, pull the plug on the stereo, and say, "If I hear another word out of you, I will take away the car keys. Now stay in your room until your dad gets home."
D. Take several deep breaths as you walk up the stairs and pray. Open the door and signal the music to be turned down. In a calm voice, say, "You know I can't allow you to speak to your sister that way. You need to apologize to your sister when you calm down. I also sense something else is going on . . ." Listening and wise punishment follow.

"D" is quite obviously the best choice, and hopefully your son would be open to talking about the frustration he feels.

We are not in charge of our kids' responses, but we are in charge of ours. If we remain calm and look past the surface behavior, we can begin to help our kids recognize and manage their anger. Our biggest challenge as parents during this time is to maintain self-control so we don't end up in a match of the emotions. No one wins when both of you are out of control. One of you must remain firm, calm, and understanding—and that one needs to be you.

Here are a few ideas to help you respond to your teenagers with insight rather than react to the surface expressions.

• Listen before making demands and assumptions.

- Ask understanding questions.
- Reassure them of your love.
- Verbally reaffirm their strengths.
- Look at them with eyes of love, not of anger.
- Never laugh at or demean your teen.
- Calm your teens down but don't shut them up.
- Let them know you desire to understand.
- Use a gentle yet firm tone when disciplining.
- Make sure they understand why they are being disciplined.

Your teens are signaling to you they are in need of understanding. Continually deal with the anger they are expressing, so it doesn't build up inside them. Never say, "I don't want to hear it!" If your child is out of control, allow him time to regain his composure then help him identify his anger. If he asks why he has to obey a certain rule, try not to respond, "Because I told you so." This tends to breed more anger. Teens may not seem rational, but they are learning to be logical. As often as possible, give your children a logical reason or explanation as to why you have set certain rules or boundaries. It's okay to say, "Because I love you and want the best for you."

Let's determine to see the best in our teens, and not assume the worst.

You may find it helpful to make yourself little reminder cards that say, "Look past the surface behavior and into the heart." Place them in strategic places in order to help you in the heat of the moment. It's not easy to respond rather than react. We need God's gracious help. Let's admit that it is downright hard to stay calm when our teen is out of control. The fruit of God's spirit is love, joy, peace, patience, kindness, goodness, faithfulness, gentleness, and self-control. We all need a few of those qualities as we are dealing with teens, don't we?

Our Humble Recognition

Let's determine to see the best in our teens, not assume the worst. These are years that can be filled with growth and joy and enrichment as our kids mature and prepare to leave the nest. They can be glorious years of personal spiritual growth as our kids begin to develop their faith through their personal prayer time and discovery of God's Word. We can also begin to help our teens develop from a self-centered mentality to an others-focused mentality. Yes, it can happen. Trust what God can do with their precious learning hearts and provide opportunities for them to serve and reach out to others.

Encourage healthy discussions around the dinner table and look for ways to build each other up. Yes, parenting teens takes time, thought, care, and prayer, but it can lead to some of the most blessed bonding times in your relationships as well. Perhaps one reason parents dread the teen years is because there are no clear-cut answers on how to handle the challenges we face during this time. We are stretched, we are humbled, and we learn to rely on the Lord.

Have you ever thought that God may be using the teen years of parenting to mature you as well? In his book *Age of Opportunity*, Paul David Tripp says, "These years are hard for us because they rip back the curtain and expose us. This is why trials are so difficult, yet so useful in God's hands. We don't radically change in a moment of trial. No, trials expose what we have always been. Trials bare things to which we would have otherwise been blind. So, too, the teen years expose our self-righteousness, our impatience, our unforgiving spirit, our lack of servant love, the weakness of our faith, and our craving for comfort and ease."[6]

And so our kids' teen years change us and grow us as well. They help us see that we are not perfect, and we have weaknesses and faults. We need the Lord each step of the way. Tim Kimmel, in his book *Why Christian Kids Rebel,* agrees. "Your willingness to acknowledge your own feet of clay is one of the best starting points when it comes to helping your children, especially when they have chosen to embrace an attitude of rebellion against you, or God, or both. A realistic view of ourselves forces us to lean on God and helps us look at our rebellious children through His loving and grace-filled eyes."[7]

Leaning on God is a good thing! What a blessed example for our young people to see—not a perfect parent, but one who humbly relies on God.

Love Notes from God

They refused to listen and did not remember the miracles you had done for them. Instead, they rebelled and appointed a leader to take them back to their slavery in Egypt! But you are a God of forgiveness, gracious and merciful, slow to become angry, and full of unfailing love and mercy. You did not abandon them, even though they made an idol shaped like a calf and said, "This is your god who brought you out of Egypt!" They sinned and committed terrible blasphemies. But in your great mercy you did not abandon them to die in the wilderness. The pillar of cloud still led them forward by day, and the pillar of fire showed them the way through the night. You sent your good Spirit to instruct them, and you did not stop giving them bread from heaven or water for their thirst. For forty years you sustained them in the wilderness. They lacked nothing in all that time. Their clothes did not wear out, and their feet did not swell! (Neh. 9:17–21NLT)

God certainly knows what it is like to raise a difficult child. Although He provided for the Israelites, they turned from Him. Yet because of His merciful and unfailing love, He did not abandon them.

That same love pours out to us and our teens today. God is gracious and merciful, slow to become angry, and full of unfailing love and mercy. Truly we can rejoice in so great a love. He is our provider and sustainer. He loved us through our rebellion and sin, and He loves our teens as well. May His gracious love overflow from our hearts and cover our teens.

■ ■ ■

How does it help me to recognize God's gracious mercy toward my sin?

How can I help my child to understand and receive His unfailing love?

How to Respond to Your Spouse's Anger

Finally, my brethren, be strong in the Lord
and in the power of His might.
—EPHESIANS 6:10 NKJV

There is no estate to which Satan is
more opposed as to marriage.
—MARTIN LUTHER

Several years ago, I had the privilege of meeting Hannah (not her real name) during a retreat at which I was speaking. She was a precious, sweet-natured woman with a deep and abiding love for the Lord. Hannah tearfully shared her story with me after we met. She grew up in a Christian home and loved the Lord ever since she was a little girl. She didn't date much in high school, but when she went to college she met the man of her dreams. Handsome, godly, and kind, he seemed to be Mr. Right in Hannah's eyes. They married after graduation, but the fairy-tale marriage soon revealed a dark side.

A part of her husband's personality that she had never seen began to surface during the honeymoon. This once kind and loving man whom Hannah thought she knew began shouting at her and demanding her to do menial tasks for him, all in the name of Christian submission. His verbal abuse soon turned into physical abuse. After several instances of trying to explain away the bruises on her arms and face to the people at church, Hannah realized that she needed to take measures to keep herself safe. She had been living a lie, trying to maintain a "good Christian couple" image since her husband was a deacon in the church.

One day, Hannah opened her Bible to Isaiah and read these soothing words:

> But now, O Israel, the LORD who created you says: "Do not be afraid, for I have ransomed you. I have called you by name; you are mine. When you go through deep waters and great trouble, I will be with you. When you go through rivers of difficulty, you will not drown! When you walk through the fire of oppression, you will not be burned up; the flames will not consume you. For I am the LORD, your God, the Holy One of Israel, your Savior . . . you are precious to me. You are honored, and I love you. Do not be afraid, for I am with you . . ." (43:1–5 NLT).

These words comforted her like a warm embrace, and she recognized how sincerely loved she was by God.

For the more than twenty years Hannah had been in this abusive marriage, she thought God did not see her situation or her pain. She mistakenly felt as though God wanted her to submit to her husband's cruel demands and brutality. Due to her own low self-esteem, Hannah felt as though her husband's anger was her fault and in some way she deserved the punishment. She finally moved out and only agreed to come back if her husband would go to counseling with her and make a permanent change in how he dealt with his anger.

You may not be experiencing physical or verbal abuse as Hannah did, but perhaps you are enduring or dancing around your husband's anger. In this chapter, we will grow to understand some of the possible sources of his anger and recognize that although you may be the recipient of his angry outbursts, you may not be the root of his anger. We will also look at wise and healthy ways to respond to his anger.

I want to make it clear from the start, if you and/or your children are in physical danger due to your husband's anger, please seek a safe place immediately and get the help you need. You can ask a trusted friend or pastor to help you find a safe place and sound biblical counseling, or you can call 1-800-600-SAFE.

Roots of His Anger

Every man is different, so I don't want to lump all husbands in the same category or give them all the same diagnosis. On the other hand, there are some common characteristics in men that seem to generate their anger. In their book *Boiling Point,* authors Stephen Arterburn and David Stoop speak to the growing problem of men's anger in the twenty-first century. "Men today are angry. Their anger is deep seated and, like their other emotions, carefully guarded and controlled most of the time. They may not know why they're angry. They may even deny that they are angry. But they're ticked off, seething, boiling deep inside."[1]

It may seem as if your husband's anger is toward you, but often it goes much deeper to past hurts or may stem from current frustrations. Let's explore some of the reasons men are angry. This is not intended for you to use to psychoanalyze your husband but rather to gain a little more insight and understanding of who he is and what may be going on inside him.

Studies now show one of the primary sources of anger within

men stems from the lack of a fatherly influence or positive mentor. Whether the father was not a part of the family dynamics or he was often absent, some men struggle with the fact they received little or no affirmation or encouragement from their fathers. If they are not able to forgive and move on, they can allow bitterness and anger to fester inside. Some men carry childhood pain, hurt, and unmet needs all the way to their adult years (sometimes without realizing it), and it ends up spewing out, separating them from the ones they most dearly love.

Another source of anger in some men is that they base much of their self-worth on their accomplishments. As I'm sure you have noticed, many men are achievement oriented, whether it is work, hobbies, or sports. When they fall short of what they want to achieve or lose a job or don't get a promotion, they can become disappointed, frustrated, and angry. Also, our husbands deeply desire to be respected by us, and if they feel they are constantly letting us down, they can also feel an intense frustration and anger.

Few men learned how to properly handle their anger during their growing-up years. Some men were encouraged to hide or stuff their anger, thereby learning to repress or suppress it. Other men learned to express their anger in a violent or destructive manner because they saw their fathers handle anger this way, or they were never corrected and shown how to express their anger in a positive way. Some men learned to handle their anger by blaming others and rarely taking ownership or responsibility for their own actions or anger. Unfortunately, those men are still blaming others, only now it is their bosses, their wives, or their circumstances.

Very few men express their anger in a healthy way by recognizing it and choosing to handle it constructively. We may not be able to change our husbands' ways of expressing anger, but we can choose to respond in a way that encourages them toward positive pathways instead of destructive ones.

Don't lose hope. Remember, we all struggle with expressing our anger constructively, so let's consider our roles as helpmates, not nags and not victims.

Wise Responses

A loving wife can be a great asset to a man as she helps him work through some of his underlying anger issues. Arterburn and Stoop say, "More than anything, he needs to know that you are on his side, that you're not against him. You need to communicate, more than you probably think necessary, that you accept him and love him, even though you may not be satisfied with some of his behaviors or responses. Separate the actions from the man, and affirm the man. His search for peace may begin sooner if he knows that you are satisfied with him and willing to walk with him through the steps of healing."[2]

Here are a few key action steps we can implement as wives.

Pray. In the Bible we read, "Confess your trespasses to one another, and pray for one another, that you may be healed. The effective, fervent prayer of a righteous man [person] avails much" (James 5:16 NKJV). God continually calls us to prayer throughout His Word. Prayer benefits us as well as our husbands. As we fervently commit our husbands' anger to prayer, we place the burden on God. It helps us to step away from being our husbands' *holy spirit*; instead, we look to the only One who can change hearts. Not only can we pray for the way our husbands handle anger, but we also can pray for wisdom and discernment on how we should respond to them. Prayer takes us humbly before God and helps us to realize our own weaknesses and dependence on God.

Respect Him. A husband needs to know his wife respects him. By respecting your husband, you are not saying it is okay for him to lash out toward you in anger. Instead, you are communicating, "I believe you are above this type of behavior, and I believe you can learn to handle your anger appropriately." Respect is not condescending. Respect treats your husband as a creation of God, not as a hopeless failure. Respect doesn't mean we cower to every thing he blasts at us, but rather we stand up for ourselves and hold on to truth. We show our husbands respect by speaking in a calm and dignified tone with composure and strength. Often (but not always), genuine respect begets respect.

> Respect treats your husband as a creation of God, not as a hopeless failure.

When we treat our husbands with a calm respect, they are much more likely to respond with respect.

Affirm What He Is Doing Right. Look for something your husband is doing well (even if it is a small thing), and affirm him in it. Let him know you appreciate his hard work. Let him know you see his good qualities. We all need that affirmation at times especially when we are in the midst of a frustrating situation. As you set the tone of affirmation in your home, it can begin to relieve some of the tension.

Discuss the Frustration. Ask your husband if he wants to talk about what is frustrating him. Remember, many men simply will not talk about it. You know the personality of your husband. Some men are willing to discuss issues, while others will only feel hounded if you ask questions. You can usually sense if your husband is willing to talk, so use your discernment about helping him open up.

I'll add an additional thought here about humor. Just as humor can defuse your anger when you are about to explode, you and your husband may find an opportunity to laugh together about something that could have potentially been a trigger to anger. Now be careful; no one likes it when someone makes light of something they deeply care about. And don't use sarcasm or in any way make your husband think you are making fun of him. But used carefully, appropriate humor at the right time can lighten the situation.

Express to Him How His Anger Makes You Feel. At a time when your husband is calm, tell him that his yelling hurts you and makes you feel unloved. Do this in a gentle and respectful way. Respond to his accusations with truth. For instance, if he yells and belittles you because you forgot to take the laundry to the cleaners, say to him kindly and firmly, "It makes me feel belittled when you talk to me that way. I have many things to remember in running this household, and I'm only human. I know your clean shirts are important to you, and I'm sorry I forgot. Let's think together about how we can work out a solution." Then work together to figure out a way to trigger your memory so you won't forget, or work out a compromise that he takes his shirts to the cleaners sometimes.

Talking calmly, frankly, and honestly while working together toward a solution builds a relationship, whereas hurt feelings and anger get you nowhere.

Talking calmly, frankly, and honestly while working together toward a solution builds a relationship, whereas hurt feelings and anger get you nowhere. Some men yell at their wives when they are actually mad at someone else. Help your husband recognize where his real anger should be directed, helping him also see you are on his side and not his enemy.

Set Wise Boundaries. By setting boundaries with your husband, you are making it clear: "There are certain lines I can not allow you to cross in the way you express your anger toward me." In their book *Boundaries,* Henry Cloud and John Townsend offer this example of confronting a yelling spouse. Instead of saying, "Stop yelling at me. You must be nicer," give a firm and specific boundary to your husband such as, "You can continue to yell if you choose to. But I will choose not to be in your presence when you act that way."[3] Remember we are not in control of our husbands' behavior, but we are in control of our response. When we use healthy boundaries, "we execute the power we do have, and we stop trying to wield the power no one has," say Cloud and Townsend.[4]

Be Patient. Your husband didn't develop his poor anger management overnight, and it may take him time to form new habits. Continue to persevere through prayer, respect, affirmation, encouragement, understanding, boundaries, and healthy discussion. You may want to visit a wise, biblically based counselor if you sense your husband's anger issues are deep-seated and may need professional help.

Some Don'ts

Now that we have learned a few proactive steps, let's take a look at a few behaviors to steer away from in our quest to deal wisely with our spouses' anger.

Don't Nag. Nagging is reminding your husband over and over again about how he falls short of your needs and expectations. It may be as simple as taking out the garbage, or it may be as large as you want him to work harder to buy you a new house. I encourage you to discuss your concerns with your husband in a respectful way, but nagging about his shortcomings will only fuel the fire of his anger. Nagging rarely accomplishes anything positive and usually creates a distance of frustration and misunderstanding between you.

If you have an ongoing concern, tell the Lord continually, but don't keep repeating it to your husband.

Don't Point the Finger in Blame. When we waste our energy blaming our husbands, we become stifled in moving toward solutions. Throwing blame on our husbands only increases their levels of frustration. Be careful with phrases such as "you always" or "you never." Instead, begin looking at solutions you can work on as a couple or individually. Most importantly, take the situation to our all-knowing heavenly Father, who can give you direction in your circumstances despite your husband's faults.

Don't Be a Victim. Many angry men seek out women who have a gentle, sweet spirit because they are easily dominated and abused. You can still be gentle and sweet, yet strong and firm in not allowing him to cross certain lines. Again, if your husband is physically abusing you or the kids, leave and find a safe place. Don't confuse submission with being a victim. Submission is placing yourself voluntarily under your husband's authority as he submits to Christ. Being a victim means your husband is abusing his place of authority and unlovingly demanding you to act a certain way or forcing you to serve him for his own selfish intent.

Don't Fix His Messes. When your husband wreaks havoc by his inappropriate expressions of anger, you may be tempted to sweep up after his angry outbursts. But he needs to be responsible for his own actions. He should experience the consequences of his behavior in order to learn, grow, and change. If his anger got him into trouble at work, then don't try to smooth it over and help him get his job back. If he exploded to his mother on the phone, don't apologize for him. He is responsible for the consequences of his own behavior and must grow up.

The only time you may want to step in is when your husband's anger has been damaging to the kids. In this case, I suggest you mediate a discussion after everyone has calmed down or help your children understand that their father's anger is not against them personally, thereby helping prevent a root of bitterness in your kids. If your husband is angry due to alcohol or another addiction, I encourage you to begin visiting an Alcoholics Anonymous (Al-Anon) meeting in your area.[5] Even if your husband does not recognize his addiction, the meetings can help you find wise ways to respond without enabling him.

> You are not to blame for your husband's abusive behavior. He is the one who is choosing to react in a destructive way.

Don't Deliberately Agitate. Sometimes we may unwittingly press our husbands' hot buttons. Now, don't let him blame you for his anger. I'm not saying to dance around him on tiptoes so as to not arouse the angry giant. He is still responsible for his response, but as much as possible, it is a good idea for you to recognize and avoid certain hot buttons. As women, we often like to dig in on areas we know will make our husbands hot under the collar. We must do a self-check on our own hearts and be careful not to make spiteful, underhanded comments that may bring out the worst in them.

Don't Blame Yourself for His Anger. Often an angry man will try to make the wife feel like she is totally to blame for his unhealthy expressions of anger. He is not willing to own up to the responsibility of his own anger management, so he blames it on you. Perhaps you didn't meet his expectations in cleaning the house or maybe you made a mistake with the bills. You are human. Recognize it and forgive yourself (even if he doesn't seem to be able to forgive you). Even if you said something you shouldn't have, you are responsible for your words and actions, but he is responsible for his words and actions.

Certainly say you are sorry when necessary, but don't accept verbal or physical abuse. You are not to blame for your husband's abusive behavior. He is the one who is choosing to react in a destructive way.

Don't Use Too Many Words. Chose your words carefully, and choose your time of discussion wisely. A short discussion that stays on point is much more effective than going in all directions with fifteen different points you want to make. Keep your conversation with your husband succinct. Bringing up a sensitive issue right before bedtime is not a good idea because your husband is tired and you may be more sensitive. If you know you need to discuss an issue with your husband, decide carefully what you are going to say, then ask your husband if there is a good time for you to talk.

A Word About Emotional Abuse

We must also recognize the possible presence of emotional abuse with an angry spouse. Emotional abuse is not as easily identified as physical abuse in a home. Generally speaking, one can readily recognize and identify physical abuse, but emotional abuse tends to be less tangible and plays out in different ways according to the abuser.

Springtide Resources provides the following definition: "Emotional abuse is the repeated use of controlling and harmful behaviors by a partner to control a woman. As a result of emotional abuse, a woman lives her life in fear and repeatedly alters her thoughts, feelings, and behaviors, and denies her needs, to avoid further abuse."[6]

Now, please don't begin labeling your husband's anger as emotional abuse too quickly. Two key words in identifying emotional abuse in the definition above are "repeated" and "ongoing." If you live in constant fear of his anger or are continually concerned about what will happen if you "step out of line," please contact a counselor, mentor, or friend with whom you can talk and gain perspective on the issue.

Some people are quick to use "emotional abuse" as an excuse for divorce. I believe we must be careful here. Identifying an emotional abuser does not necessarily mean a ticket out the door. There are all different degrees and levels of this type of abuse. It is possible to begin taking steps toward healing in your marriage and helping your husband change directions. Carefully and prayerfully seek the Lord's help and redemption in your situation.

If you suspect you are living in an emotionally abusive situation, I urge you to do the following:

- Seek help and guidance from a godly counselor, mentor, or friend. Find someone who will be available for you to call and pray together when you are struggling or when you need advice. Protect your children from emotional abuse through wise counsel and help.
- Respond to your husband without lowering yourself to his level of anger or control tactics. Don't play his game but respond with firmness, wisdom, and self-respect. Abusers look for victims, so don't be one. Often an emotional abusive husband will make his wife feel like his anger is her fault. Plan a gentle but firm response to his accusations so you are able to respond with dignity.
- Don't play the martyr. Sometimes it is easier to blame your husband than to take positive steps of action for yourself. Look for what you can do. What glimmer of hope has God provided? Build on it. Continue to grow as a person and be the wonderful woman God has created you to be. Recognize God's love and care for you.

Seek help before seeking to get out of an emotionally abusive situation. Remember that God is able to do far more than we can ask or imagine. Keep looking to Him for direction. Walk in wisdom, not as a victim but as a precious child of God. Remember He is the God who sees all. You may want to reflect on the story of Hagar in Genesis 16 to see God's help and hope in the life of a woman who was despised and endured emotional and verbal abuse. God has not left you; He will help you and lead you.

Our Hard Part

You may be thinking, *But what about him? Why is it all up to me?* We must remember we are not in charge of our husbands' actions or responses; we are only in charge of our own. Certainly our responses can help lead them in new and positive directions, but positive change is up to them (and God), not us. All we can do is what is in our power to do. We need to respond rightly even if they are not acting rightly. And yes, only in God's strength and through His love can we do our part.

I encourage you to fix your eyes on Jesus and not on your husband's problems. No husband is perfect, and many do not handle their anger in a healthy and positive way. You can help bring out the best in your husband, but you can also fuel the worst in him. Take your eyes off of his shortcomings and put them on to the Lord, who can strengthen you and do a great work in his life as well as your own.

Certainly you wouldn't want your husband continually focusing on your faults, so don't do the same to him. Lovingly lift him up to be a better person. Your marriage may not be perfect, and your husband may not be kind and sensitive to all of your feelings—but perhaps God is refining you through the process. What does God want to do in your life and through your marriage? Keep your eyes turned to God, seeking His strength in your responses and His wisdom in your boundaries.

Rely on God's Strength

Life may seem unfair. Your husband doesn't handle his anger well, and you're supposed to respond with a calm strength. Dear sister, rely on God's strength, not your own to help you respond to your husband with dignity. Remember what beautiful gold comes through refinement.

May the Lord teach us, strengthen us, and grow us in His beauty and grace as we rely on Him and find our sufficiency in Him. As much as it lies with us, may we be helpmates to our husbands, helping them make positive changes as they see our wise and respectful behavior.

Love Notes from God

O God, You are my God;
Early will I seek You;
My soul thirsts for You;
My flesh longs for You
In a dry and thirsty land
Where there is no water.
So I have looked for You in the sanctuary,
To see Your power and Your glory.

Because Your lovingkindness is better than life,
My lips shall praise You.
Thus I will bless You while I live;
I will lift up my hands in Your name.
My soul shall be satisfied as with marrow and fatness,
And my mouth shall praise You with joyful lips.

When I remember You on my bed,
I meditate on You in the night watches.
Because You have been my help,
Therefore in the shadow of Your wings I will rejoice.
My soul follows close behind You;
Your right hand upholds me. (Ps. 63:1–8 NKJV)

In the shadow of His wings, we find comfort and rest. What a beautiful picture of safety: nestled in God's mighty and powerful wings. The Lord is our rock and He is our keeper. His right hand holds us up.

Run to Him, for His loving-kindness is better than life. He is able to satisfy your soul's desire for love and security. Aren't you thankful for a gracious and kind God who covers you with His love?

■ ■ ■

In what ways have I seen God sustain me in my life and in my marriage?

Create an Environment Where Love Abounds

Most important of all, continue to show deep love for each other,
for love covers a multitude of sins.

—1 PETER 4:8 NLT

It's not how much you do,
but how much love you put into what you do that counts.

—MOTHER TERESA

Our home is a classroom filled with life lessons, teaching its members how to love with a genuine, graceful love. Our education comes not from pleasant situations and perfect people; rather, we learn sincere love through people's rough spots and imperfections.

Portrait of a Loving Family

And the most important piece of clothing you must wear is love.
Love is what binds us all together in perfect harmony.
—COLOSSIANS 3:14 NLT

There is no doubt that it is around the family and the home
that all the greatest virtues, the most dominating virtues
of human society are created, strengthened, and maintained.
—WINSTON CHURCHILL

Take a moment to imagine what a loving family looks like.
You may be picturing a family who speaks kindly to one
another and smiles at each other. Perhaps you see them sitting
pleasantly around the dinner table, laughing and sharing stories, with
everyone pleasantly listening and waiting their turns to speak. Your picture of a loving family may include kids agreeably helping with chores
and sharing toys and helping each other without even asking.

Did your picture include an annoying little brother who unmerci-
fully pesters his older sister or arguments about whose turn it is to
set the table or family vacations where everyone has his own idea of
what fun looks like? I didn't think so. Although we would love to
hang our imagined family portraits on the walls of our homes, reality tells us that life isn't perfect and people are not perfect. True and
sincere love is not based on easy-to-love family members; it is choosing

to love them despite their idiosyncrasies and annoyances. We may not feel so loving all the time, but love is a choice, not a happy feeling meant only for pleasant people.

Jesus taught about selfless love. He said, "Do for others as you would like them to do for you. Do you think you deserve credit merely for loving those who love you? Even the sinners do that! And if you do good only to those who do good to you, is that so wonderful? Even sinners do that much! And if you lend money only to those who can repay you, what good is that? Even sinners will lend to their own kind for a full return.

"You must be compassionate, just as your Father is compassionate" (Luke 6:31–34, 36 NLT). There is no better training ground than our families to learn how to love imperfect humans in a sincere and selfless way.

It's time to take the fantasy portrait of the perfectly loving family off the wall, and in its place put a picture of imperfect people who are learning to love each other in a Christlike, grace-filled, selfless way. The key word here is *learning*. Only through the strength of the Holy Spirit can we grow and learn to love as He does. Oh, if only we had even an ounce of God's divine love to pour out to the people around us!

Loving Our Kids So They Feel Loved

You know you love your children unconditionally. It is very clear to you, but do your kids know it? You might say, "Of course they do. I tell them I love them all the time." Yet our kids know they are loved not by hearing the words, but by receiving the actions of love. As parents, perhaps our single most important role is to continually make sure our kids know and feel they are unconditionally loved. When our kids feel secure in our love, they are more likely to show love to others—starting with their siblings.

A loving home begins at the top, with parents demonstrating a sincere love between husband and wife (we'll talk about this a little later in the chapter) and parent to child. We have a lot of responsibility! Kids often fall into the performance track of assuming they must earn our love. They think, *If I play the piano or baseball or soccer, then I get my parents' attention and love.* We need to reassure them on a regular basis that it is not what they do that makes us love them. What are some practical ways we can demonstrate love to our children? Here are a few ways to give value to our words:

> The ultimate way to demonstrate love is to serve one another.

Loving Touch. We each have different ways of showing affection. It may be a hug or a kiss or putting your arm around someone's shoulder. From infancy to teenage years and even into adulthood, our kids need to receive our embrace or touch. It is a basic human need.

Attention. We show our kids we truly care about the details of their lives by giving them our attention. Attention can come in the form of eye contact or a heart-to-heart conversation or simply time spent together. Let them know you are interested in each of your children as people, not just in what they do or accomplish. Reassure your kids that they are worth your attention, which takes time and focus.

Selfless Acts, Serving, and Sacrifice. The ultimate way to demonstrate love is to serve one another. Jesus demonstrated love to His disciples as He washed their feet, and His ultimate demonstration of love was giving His life for us. Now, we do need to bring a balance to our selfless acts, so our kids don't take advantage of our sacrifices. I've honestly seen some moms who wait on their kids to the point the kids don't do anything for themselves, which is unhealthy for the children. Yet there are many times we can voluntarily serve our families out of true love. I'll never forget the time my mother came over and completely cleaned our home while I was speaking on the other side of Dallas. I didn't ask her to; she just did it as an act of service that I remember to this day—twenty years later.

Belief, Trust, and Added Responsibility. As our kids grow and mature, we can begin to give them a little more responsibility and independence. It may be something small, such as allowing them to walk the dog around the block without your supervision, or something big, like using your car to run some errands. When we grant our children trust and responsibility, we are lovingly showing them that we trust them and believe they can accomplish things.

> Our kids know they are loved when we set wise and reasonable rules and boundaries for them.

Encouragement. We strengthen our kids through our words of encouragement. Whether we write them a note or e-mail or tell them face-to-face, we give our kids a loving gift when we give them the delicious morsels of our encouraging words. I'm not talking about superficial flattery; I'm talking about sincere and specific affirmation. "Honey, I'm so thankful for your patience this afternoon while I ran errands. You blessed me with your sweet attitude." Or "I'm so thankful God gave me a son like you. I appreciate your polite response to my instructions." Don't only affirm accomplishments such as sports or grades, but be sure to continually encourage your kids' inner qualities and character traits. If you only recognize their accomplishments, then they may wrongly begin to think that you love them only for how they perform.

Boundaries and Discipline. Our kids know they are loved when we set wise and reasonable rules and boundaries for them. This is another way of assuring them we care about them. If a mother didn't love or care for her children, she would let them run wild and do whatever they want to destroy their own lives. When we love some-one, we teach, train, and discipline them in order to help them grow to be mature and wise adults. But be careful; too many rules or over-the-top regulations can only serve to exasperate your child.

Love Between Siblings

Love in the home begins with the parents, and it trickles down into the love between siblings. How do we encourage this brotherly/sisterly love? One of the first steps is to require kind and loving inter-action between family members. As you model respect in the way you treat family members, they begin to see how it is done. So yes, as a mom, the first step is yours in setting the tone for respectful interaction.

It is important to apply discipline when there is disrespect among siblings. Your kids may argue, but they do not need to cross the lines of demeaning disrespect and rude or demeaning comments. Help them learn to appreciate the differences and to see each other as a gift from God.

If your young children are having trouble sharing an object, then use the timer to give each child ten minutes to play with the object. You may need to flip a coin to see who gets it first. Often, a child will calm down if she knows she will have her chance to play with the toy. Many times after the first ten minutes is over, the other child isn't even interested anymore and has moved on. The timer idea per-sonally helped my two daughters through many a potential battle over dolls and tea sets. With boys, you may need to put them in sep-arate rooms while they wait for the timer.

When older kids argue, it is wise to separate them in order for them to have time to settle down and calm their spirits. Once you have given them adequate time to calm down, if the issue over which they were arguing still seems to be an issue, talk to each child individually. Pray with each of them, and then bring them back together for mediation where you are the mediator. As you work through a fair solution, give the kids an opportunity to apologize for any disrespectful comments.

Most importantly, we can build love between siblings through shared experiences together. Dinnertime conversations in which you talk about each other's interests, family vacations, and supporting each other at games and performances can all serve as love builders between family members. Family meetings and/or family devotionals can also build closeness as you discuss God's Word and family values together.

One effective tool for building encouragement between family members is to share with each person in your family what you appreciate about him or her. You may want to take a series of Sunday evenings to gather as a family and choose one member of the family to encourage. Everyone must contribute. Give each member of your family an opportunity to say the qualities they appreciate most about the honoree.

Loving Through Wise Discipline

When we talk about love we must also talk about discipline, for they go hand in hand. The Bible tells us God disciplines those whom He loves (Heb. 12:6), and certainly if we love our kids we will discipline them in a wise and loving way.

In this book, we have looked at ways to train our children to handle their anger in a healthy way, but here we want to touch on how to employ loving discipline in the home. We will only cover the topic briefly here. I recommend the following books on parenting and discipline: *Shepherding a Child's Heart* by Tedd Tripp, *How to Really Parent Your Child* by Dr. Ross Campbell, and *Grace-Based Parenting* by Dr. Tim Kimmel.[1]

When kids are unruly, disobedient, disrespectful, or just plain childish and silly, our ire can be raised in seconds. If we want our children's behavior to change, then the best solution is to be wise in the discipline we administer to our children. In order to be effective, our discipline must be handled with calm discernment, not reckless aggression. If necessary, take a minute (or longer) to regain your composure.

The word *discipline* means "to teach." How can we effectively teach or train our children in a new behavior and curb the old one? First, make the discipline painful so it will curb the behavior. Don't send your child to her room if she likes hanging out there anyway. Think about an activity or item your child truly enjoys, and consider taking the privilege away for a reasonable time period.

Second, use natural consequences as often as possible. If your child storms in the house, slamming the door so hard that the window breaks, then the child should work to earn enough money to pay for the broken window. If your child disobeys one of your rules while visiting a friend, then a natural consequence is he cannot visit that friend for a certain time period. Be sure to set reasonable time limits so you don't extend the punishment to the point that you have forgotten what it is for. Short and painful is much more effective than long and light.

Third, discuss the punishment with your child. Make sure he understands why he is being punished and the importance of learning the lesson. Even at a young age, kids can understand the difference between right and wrong. Calmly tell your child that because you love him, you want to help him learn right from wrong. Screaming a useless punishment at your child doesn't have the same long-term gain.

Love Learned by Example

Our kids learn to love and respect others as they see it modeled in the home. It begins with you! Now here's the even harder statement to swallow: it begins with you showing respect to your husband. *Uh-oh,* you may be thinking, *I haven't done such a good job in that area.* Don't be hard on yourself, but begin today recognizing that you set the tone and example of how to sincerely love and show respect to others. Like it or not, your children are watching you and learning from you. Please don't point your finger at your husband and say, "But he . . ." Remember, you are not in control of how your husband demonstrates love. This book is about you, and you are in charge of your actions.

Making cutting comments under your breath, yelling at him, or saying things to your husband in a rude and demeaning tone teach your kids to be disrespectful to others (especially to their future spouses). If you have struggled in this area, make a commitment right now that from this point forward, you will seek God's help in being a loving and respectful example.

Every person—even your husband!—is a creation of God and is deserving of respect. Yes, you may see your husband's glaring faults as bigger than life, but he is a creation of God and deserves respect. Isn't it peculiar how we can treat perfect strangers with more respect than we do our spouses? Check your tone even on the phone. Love and respect him through your tone of voice, and you may discover him showing loving respect back to you. As Martin Walsh says, "When you look for the good in others you discover the best in yourself."[2]

The apostle Paul encourages us, "Let the wife see that she respects her husband" (Eph. 5:33 NKJV). Ask God to give you a new love and respect for your husband. Focus on his finer qualities, and choose to overlook some of the areas that tend to annoy you. Do it to bless not only your marriage but also your children.

> There is no match for God's great love for us.

If you are divorced, you can still show respect to your ex. I know this may seem impossible, but prayerfully seek God's help and wisdom in how to show kindness to your ex-husband, even though you don't believe he deserves it. I know you have been hurt, but help your kids understand the principles of love, forgiveness, and respect as they see you model them in your relationship with your former husband. Remember, love is not simply loving the lovely. Jesus calls us to love our enemies and those who are not so easy to love.

As our children see God's gracious love pour forth from our hearts, they learn how to love others, beginning with their siblings. As we all know, loving others doesn't come naturally. We need God. We need to know and savor His great love for us, and we need His power to love people through us. There is no match for God's great love for us. Relish it, dwell in it, enjoy it, and allow it to splash over from your life and refresh those around you.

Love Notes from God

Therefore, since we have been made right in God's sight by faith, we have peace with God because of what Jesus Christ our Lord has done for us. Because of our faith, Christ has brought us into this place of highest privilege where we now stand, and we confidently and joyfully look forward to sharing God's glory.

We can rejoice, too, when we run into problems and trials, for we know that they are good for us—they help us learn to endure. And endurance develops strength of character in us, and character strengthens our confident expectation of salvation. And this expectation will not disappoint us. For we know how dearly God loves us, because he has given us the Holy Spirit to fill our hearts with his love.

When we were utterly helpless, Christ came at just the right time and died for us sinners. Now, no one is likely to die for a good person, though someone might be willing to die for a person who is especially good. But God showed his great love for us by sending Christ to die for us while we were still sinners. And since we have been made right in God's sight by the blood of Christ, he will certainly save us from God's judgment. (Rom. 5:1–9 NLT)

God demonstrated His perfect love for us when He sent Jesus to die on the cross. While we were yet sinners, God provided forgiveness and redemption. We didn't deserve it, yet He sacrificed His only Son on our behalf. What amazing love!

My friend, do you know God's abundant love for you? You are a cherished child. With a thankful heart, dwell today on the beauty of His love for you. Each and every day, remember His gracious loving-kindness toward you. And as you do, ask His Spirit to pour that love through you to your family.

■ ■ ■

How do I demonstrate a merciful and gracious love toward my family members?

13

Teaching Your Kids Genuine Compassion

My little children, let us not love in word or in tongue,
but in deed and in truth.
—1 JOHN 3:18 NKJV

You will find as you look back upon your life
that the moments that stand out, the moments when you have really lived,
are the moments when you have done things in a spirit of love.
—HENRY DRUMMOND

*O*f you want to have a happy, almost euphoric feeling inside, do something for someone else. That's right! If you are having a bad day, lift up someone else and you will be lifted up as well. It's one thing to read about the joy of showing compassion to another person; it is another thing to experience it yourself. I can tell you from personal experience that the best way to get rid of the grumbles (whether yours or your kids') is to reach out in love and serve others. As we learn the joy of service, we can teach it to our families.

Not too long ago on a Saturday morning, I was feeling regret for signing up to serve at the local Special Olympics softball and bocce ball tournament. There were about twenty million other things I needed to accomplish that day, but I had signed up along with my teenage daughters, and we had to keep our commitment. My girls weren't so thrilled about our obligation either. As we arrived, we were assigned to three different bocce ball games. Of course we had a little bit of a learning curve because we had never even heard of the game, much less played it—and now we were helping to score!

The more important part of the job was to encourage, hug, and help the participants. We learned, we helped, and we cheered. We were surrounded by loving people of all ages, sizes, races, and degrees of physical challenge. The joy and enthusiasm of the Special Olympics participants was contagious. Soon we were all smiles as we opened our loving arms to our new friends. The car ride back home was filled with a different emotion than when we drove to the event. Our spirits were jovial as we shared stories of the precious people we had encountered and how they each enriched our hearts.

I wouldn't trade that Saturday morning for the world. Money can't buy a life lesson like this one. That day, my daughters and I experienced the true joy that comes from giving, not from receiving or taking. As a mom, I could have told my daughters until I was blue in the face, "It is more blessed to give than to receive." But they got the message loud and clear by doing it. As a family we have taken other opportunities to feed the homeless, work at the Angel Tree at the mall, and visit families in need, and we have been enriched with joy every time.

What have my kids learned through the process? The proof is in their choices as they now share love and compassion with others on their own accord. Currently my daughters are in college, and they are serving others in their college-area communities, without my prodding. Compassion is often caught rather than taught.

Compassion means more than just caring; it means stepping out of our comfort zones and reaching out to lend a hand. Through church, school, friends, and charitable organizations, we all have numerous opportunities to serve others; we just have to make the decision to do it.

Give and It Will Be Given Back to You

Jesus said, "Give, and it will be given to you: good measure, pressed down, shaken together, and running over will be put into your bosom. For with the same measure that you use, it will be measured back to you" (Luke 6:38 NKJV). Perhaps you have heard this passage used in a sermon concerning financial giving, but Jesus wasn't talking about finances here. If we look at the context, He was talking about love, mercy, and forgiveness. As we pour the beautiful qualities of love and compassion out toward others, we will receive great joy in the process.

Now I'm not saying we should reach out in compassion only because it makes us feel good. I'm simply saying there are blessings and benefits to our reaching out, and it is important for our kids to see those. As they experience the joy of touching others' lives, their love for others grows. We learn to be content with what we have when we help those who are in need. Serving others changes our hearts, our perspectives, and our interactions with others. The bottom line is we are acting out of obedience to Christ, who encouraged us to give a cup of cold water to those in need (Matt. 10:42).

> As we pour the beautiful qualities of love and compassion out toward others, we will receive great joy in the process.

What can you do to give to others? Begin by considering your own gifts and talents. If you enjoy cooking, look for opportunities to bring meals to others in need. As a family, you can prepare the meal and deliver it together. If you enjoy singing, offer to visit a nursing home or an organization that needs to hear your uplifting music. If you love helping and cheering people on, then volunteering for the Special Olympics or at a local school can be just the right thing for you and your family. Maybe your boys need the opportunity to help build a house or paint a room, so Habitat for Humanity may be the thing for you. Don't just look for ways to do what you like; allow yourself to be stretched as well. Service often demands sacrifice and is not always easy or fun.

You may want to schedule a day once a month or once a quarter designated for service. Our lives tend to get too busy, so if we don't schedule a service day on the calendar, it may not happen. We all want to serve and we have good intentions of serving, but the key is to be deliberate about it and make it happen even if it is just once or twice a year. Perhaps there is an opportunity for a local or international mission trip that you and your family could go on together.

Here's a list of a few organizations that you may consider contacting to serve:

Meals on Wheels: www.mowaa.org
Ronald McDonald House: www.rmhc.com
Salvation Army: www.salvationarmyusa.org
Habitat for Humanity: www.habitat.org
Special Olympics: www.specialolympics.org
Adventures in Missions (AIM): www.adventures.org

Please don't force your children to serve others under obligation or duress. There is a happy balance between encouraging them to serve others and forcing them to do so. Pray for God's direction and gently, lovingly stretch your kids to join you in service. Bring their friends along if it would help. Their friends will experience a blessing as well. As your kids get older, allow them to choose the places where they want to serve and go along with them. There's no greater bond for a family than serving together.

One Woman, Big Difference

Born in 1905, Clara McBride Hale grew up to be a devoted and loving mother who raised her children in the classroom of love and compassion. She not only took care of her own kids, but she reached out to many other youngsters in need. Her unconditional love for children was the catalyst that led her to open Hale House in Harlem, New York, in the early 1970s. This home for infants born to drug-addicted mothers filled a desperate need in the community. Her program provided love, nurture, and much-needed medical attention to the babies and also offered help and rehabilitation to the families.

The beautiful story of compassion didn't stop with "Mother," as Clara Hale was affectionately known. Her daughter, Dr. Lorraine Hale, went on to be the administrator for the Hale House. During his 1985 State of the Union speech, president Ronald Reagan commended Clara as an "American hero." Through her love and compassion, she became a bright light shining in her community.

Who has God placed in your path? Is it a neighbor who needs help with her yard or a friend who is suffering from a debilitating disease? Are you willing to step out of your comfort zone and touch others' lives, bringing your family with you? Reach out to touch those in need—and watch the transformation that takes place in your own family.

Love has a multiplying effect. As we give love, compassion, and mercy to others, it has a way of duplicating and growing in our own lives. As Henry Van Dyke said, "There is a loftier ambition than merely to stand high in the world. It is to stoop down and lift mankind a little higher."[1]

Love Notes from God

Dear friends, let us continue to love one another, for love comes from God. Anyone who loves is born of God and knows God. But anyone who does not love does not know God—for God is love.

God showed how much he loved us by sending his only Son into the world so that we might have eternal life through him. This is real love. It is not that we loved God, but that he loved us and sent his Son as a sacrifice to take away our sins.

Dear friends, since God loved us that much, we surely ought to love each other. (1 John 4:7–11 NLT)

God's great love for us compels us to reach out and love others. God showed His love to us through His actions. He didn't just say, "I have loved you with an everlasting love" (Jer. 31:3); He followed it up by sending His Son to die for us.

Now we, the recipients of God's great love, can share it with the world. As we reach out to touch others, we not only bless others in the name of Christ, but we also bless our own lives. In Jesus' own words, "Blessed are the merciful, for they will be shown mercy" (Matt. 5:7). We have received from God; now let us freely give to others.

■ ■ ■

In what ways am I sharing the love of Christ with others in my community through acts of compassion and service?

14

Happiness Is a Family Full of Forgiveness

Bear with each other and forgive
whatever grievances you may have against one another.
Forgive as the Lord forgave you.
—Colossians 3:13

Love lets the past die. It moves people to a new beginning
without settling the past. Love prefers to tuck the loose ends
of past rights and wrongs in the bosom of forgiveness—
and pushes us into a new start.
—Lewis B. Smedes

Have you ever seen the painted, three-dimensional, decorative wooden words sold at many gift or furniture stores? Usually they are pleasant words like *Love* or *Peace* or *Sisterhood*. One time I was walking through a store and saw several decorative words, yet one word seemed to shout at me. It was the word *Forgive*. Trust me, there was a large quantity of those words still in the store. Who wants to decorate their house with a difficult word like *Forgive* when you can buy delightful words like *Laughter, Joy,* or *Happiness?*

On a whim I bought the word *Forgive* and placed it in my kitchen. It was interesting to me to hear people's comments as they saw the word on the counter. They'd say something like, "Oh, I needed to see that today" and then tell me about a situation in which they needed to forgive another person. One time a friend came over, saw the word *Forgive,* and let out a big sigh. I asked her, "Is there someone you need to forgive?" She responded, "Well, actually I needed to be reminded to forgive myself when I beat myself up in my thought life."

I began to see how very powerful the word *forgive* is to all of us. We need the constant reminder all throughout the day. One day as another friend was walking by the ledge where I kept this powerful word, she accidentally knocked it off and broke it. You can imagine my disappointment. But I guess when someone breaks your *Forgive* sign, you need to forgive her! So of course I hugged her and told her it was all right. The next day I went back to the store and found a stack of the *Forgive* words on the table (on sale, I might add), so I just bought another one!

To most people *forgiveness* isn't an easy word, yet once we embrace it, it can be one of the sweetest words we know. Reba McEntire once said, "When I learned to forgive, it was like a million pounds were lifted from me."[1] Now that's a quick weight-loss plan! Certainly our relationships within our families benefit when we choose to release our guilt-grip on another person. But the real reason we forgive is not for our own benefit or even for the other person's benefit. The bottom-line reason to forgive is our relationship with God. Allow me to explain.

We Forgive Because God Forgives

Who among us has never sinned? Every person reading this book (plus the writer of this book) is a sinning person. Now you may be thinking, *Don't lump me together with all the bad people in the world.* Okay, so maybe you haven't robbed a bank or cheated someone out of their hard-earned money, but if we are going to be brutally honest with ourselves, we will recognize that we have a sin problem. Think about some of those little things that creep into your life every day.

I'll just name a few. Bear with me here. I'm not trying to heap guilt on our backs; instead I am trying to remind us all (including me) of the large amount of junk for which we have been forgiven by our heavenly Father. So let us ask ourselves, gently of course, have I . . .

- been jealous?
- lashed out in anger at a loved one?
- held a grudge?
- gossiped, told stories, or talked about others behind their backs?
- lied to another person?
- wallowed in self-pity or pride?
- ignored or despised another person?
- been rude, impatient, or self-seeking?
- had impure thoughts or evil desires?
- been greedy or self-centered?

And that's just the short list! Again, let this list be a reminder to rejoice in the fact that we have been forgiven much. Do not use this as an excuse to wallow in regret or dwell on your sin. Take comfort and joy in the fact that there is no condemnation for those who are in Christ Jesus. My friend, as we begin to understand the beauty of the gospel message, we realize our sins are completely forgiven through faith in Jesus and what He did on the cross. He paid the price tag for your sins and mine.[2] When we begin to grasp the significance of God's great forgiveness toward us, it changes the way we relate to others, especially the members in our families.

Pastor Ray Pritchard, in his book *The Healing Power of Forgiveness,* says, "The more you see the seriousness of your sin before God, the less the sins of other people against you will bother you."[3] If we recognize that we, too, are sinners in need of God's grace, then we must look at others in a different light. The Bible says "all have sinned and fall short of the glory of God" (Rom. 3:23). That includes you and me. Oh, how good it feels to be fully forgiven! Take a moment right now to thank the Lord for the fact that through Christ's death on the cross, your sins are forgiven. The penalty and price for your sin has been paid once and for all.

> When we begin to grasp the significance of God's great forgiveness toward us, it changes the way we relate to others, especially the members in our families.

Why is it so very important for us to understand God's forgiveness? Because when we recognize that God has forgiven us, we are motivated to forgive those around us. I love the story of when the apostle Peter asked Jesus, "Lord, how often shall my brother sin against me, and I forgive him? Up to seven times?" (Matt. 18:21 NKJV). Can't you just hear the twinge of pride in Peter's voice? *I'm pretty good for thinking about forgiving someone seven times, aren't I, Jesus?*

Jesus responded, "I do not say to you, up to seven times, but up to seventy times seven"(Matt. 18:22 NKJV). Then He told a story to help us all "get the picture" of our basis for forgiveness.

> Therefore the kingdom of heaven is like a certain king who wanted to settle accounts with his servants.
>
> And when he had begun to settle accounts, one was brought to him who owed him ten thousand talents [around a million dollars].

But as he was not able to pay, his master commanded that he be sold, with his wife and children and all that he had, and that payment be made.

The servant therefore fell down before him, saying, "Master, have patience with me, and I will pay you all."

Then the master of that servant was moved with compassion, released him, and forgave him the debt.

But that servant went out and found one of his fellow servants who owed him a hundred denarii [a couple of thousand dollars]; and he laid hands on him and took him by the throat, saying, "Pay me what you owe!"

So his fellow servant fell down at his feet and begged him, saying, "Have patience with me, and I will pay you all."

And he would not, but went and threw him into prison till he should pay the debt.

So when his fellow servants saw what had been done, they were very grieved, and came and told their master all that had been done.

Then his master, after he had called him, said to him, "You wicked servant! I forgave you all that debt because you begged me.

Should you not also have had compassion on your fellow servant, just as I had pity on you?"

And his master was angry, and delivered him to the torturers until he should pay all that was due to him.

So My heavenly Father also will do to you if each of you, from his heart, does not forgive his brother his trespasses. (Matt. 18:23–35 NKJV)

Whoa, that last statement by Jesus is pretty strong, wouldn't you say? Apparently God is pretty serious about this forgiveness issue!

Not only do we need to understand and apply the concept of forgiveness, but we also need to help our children grasp it as well. A good place to begin is to share Jesus' parable about the unforgiving servant during family discussion time or during dinner one night. It offers a wonderful way to teach our kids about the truth and blessing of forgiveness.

What Does Forgiveness Look Like?

When I think of unforgiveness, I think of a huge bag of rocks. Every time someone sins against you or hurts you or does something awful to you, you have a choice whether to forgive or to hold on to unforgiveness. If you choose unforgiveness, it is like picking up a heavy rock and placing it in a bag you are carrying over your shoulders. Some rocks are bigger than others, depending on how much you dwell on your hurt and allow it to fester and grow. By the way, the rock is not added to the offender's bag. Often the offender couldn't care less if you forgive her or not. You think you are really going to show her how much she hurt you, but really you are just adding a burden to your own life.

Forgiveness isn't saying, "It is okay for you to hurt me, and please do it again." In fact, in certain situations we must forgive as well as define clear boundaries, so the offender understands you will not allow it again. Forgiveness is an issue of the heart and mind that says, "I choose to no longer hold this offense over you." It is a decision to move forward from the incident and a conscious choice not to bring it up again. Forgiveness does not deny the pain, but it does serve as a catalyst to move you through and out of the pain. It is doing for others what God does for us. The Bible describes God's forgiveness like this: "as far as the east is from the west, so far has he removed our transgressions from us" (Ps. 103:12). Forgiveness is taking that bag of rocks and dumping it in the ocean of God's vast love and mercy. It is releasing the right to seek revenge as well.

Forgiveness is not based on whether the offender deserves it. It is not even based on whether the offender knows or feels bad about what he has done. Think of Jesus' example as He hung on the cross, praying, "Father, forgive them, for they do not know what they do" (Luke 23:34 NKJV). Forgiveness is based on the picture of God's great grace toward us. Don't get forgiveness mixed up with allowing someone to use or abuse you. And no, forgiveness doesn't mean you allow yourself to be a weak doormat.

> Forgiveness is based on the picture of God's great grace toward us.

Just as forgiveness requires prayer, so setting boundaries between you and a hurtful person requires prayer.

Seek God's wisdom and direction as to what your healthy boundaries should be. Consult a wise and godly friend, perhaps someone who has been through a similar situation. Two excellent books on lovingly setting boundaries are *Love Must Be Tough* by Dr. James Dobson and *Boundaries* by Henry Cloud and John Townsend.[4] As I have mentioned previously, if you or your children are in an abusive or harmful situation, I encourage you to seek help immediately. Do not confuse forgiveness with staying in a physically dangerous situation.

Once you have forgiven a person in your heart, often the memory of the situation or the offense will pop back into your mind. If this happens to you, I encourage you to redirect your thoughts. Reflect on God's goodness and mercy and ask for His help in not reliving the incident. Look for any glimmer of hope that may have resulted from the situation. Think about what God can do through you to turn this into a positive and bless other people. When we focus on how we can lift up others (sometimes through our pain), we get our eyes off ourselves and our hurts and discover that our spirits are lifted as well.

Let's review the steps to forgiveness we have learned so far:

1. Reflect on your own need for forgiveness.
2. Recognize the offender is a fellow sinner in need of forgiveness.
3. Refuse to hold the offense over the other person.
4. Release the need to let the offender know how much he hurt you.
5. Realize you are obeying God as you make a conscious decision to forgive.
6. Rely on God to help you to sincerely forgive the person.
7. Replace the memories with new truth. After you grieve the hurt and pain incurred, move on.
8. Respond with healthy boundaries if necessary.

Our kids benefit and move forward in their lives as they learn the beautiful principle of forgiveness. Many kids must practice forgiveness on a daily basis when it comes to issues with friends or problems with parents or teachers. Situations arise continually within a family between siblings. Once we understand the purpose and principles of forgiveness, we release the "bag of rocks" of our potential bitterness. Let's begin with our own example of forgiving others, and then as teachable moments arise, let's encourage our children and teens down the joyful pathway of forgiveness.

Forgiving When It Seems Impossible

Maybe you've been wronged unfairly, and the hurt is too painful. Perhaps your child has been hurt or wounded emotionally or physically by another person. Your life circumstances may have been altered due to someone else's poor choice or immoral action or foolish mistake. The issue may be still very raw and sensitive. How can you forgive? Is it even possible? Yes, as the Bible tells us, "with God all things are possible" (Matt. 19:26). And that's where we begin—with God.

Let's not ignore the fact that we are hurt. We have experienced a deep, perhaps life-altering pain, and we must grieve. Forgiving doesn't mean we ignore the pain and move on. It means we cry and grieve the loss or hurt, and then from the pit of despair we look to God. In our pain, we must cry out to God and recognize He is sovereign, He loves us, and He has not left us. In fact, I believe the only way we can endure suffering and experience the transforming power of forgiveness is by recognizing that our loving God holds us in His arms and by relying on His power, presence, and strength to see us through.

Although it may be hard to accept or comprehend at times, the Bible is clear that God is sovereign. He is the God who knows all things, sees all things, and is able to do all things; therefore, He is well aware of your circumstances. He not only knows what is going on, but He also is able to work something good through the awful circumstances. Although you may not be able to even imagine anything good that could come from this situation, He is able to do far more than you could ever ask or imagine (Eph. 3:20). Yes, you can trust God to take care of your kids through this challenge in life as well.

Perhaps you are mad at God, and it is God whom you need to forgive. My friend, you are not alone. Please know that many have struggled shaking their fists heavenward, shouting "Why?!" Bring your heartache to God. Job did and eventually realized he couldn't figure out God and His ways.

He who created the smallest atom and the grandest of solar systems cannot be fully understood. We may not understand His ways, but we can trust His love. The Bible says: "'For My thoughts are not your thoughts, nor are your ways My ways,' says the LORD. 'For as the heavens are higher than the earth, so are My ways higher than your ways, and My thoughts than your thoughts'" (Isa. 55:8–9 NKJV).

Are you willing to turn your heart toward a loving God and say, "Lord, I can't see it now, but I know You are able to make something beautiful out of this rubble. I believe You love me, even though Your ways don't always make sense to me. Help me and lead me to a place of forgiveness, recognizing that You love me and are able to hold me through these difficult times. My life is in Your hands."

> When we lay our requests before the Lord and teach our children to do the same, He will answer us.

When we lay our requests before the Lord and teach our children to do the same, He will answer us. It may not be exactly the answer we want, but He will give us what we need day by day. The pathway to healing begins when we recognize our need for God's loving hands to hold us. Then, by His help and strength, we are able to move to a place of forgiveness. As we forgive others, we take the first steps out of the pit and onto the road of hope and possibilities. Trust Him and encourage your family to trust Him day by day.

The Sobering Seriousness of Forgiveness

Consider this: How much of your sin has God forgiven? Three-tenths? Two-fifths? One-half? If you have placed your faith in Christ as your sin bearer, the One who paid the penalty for your sin, then there is only one answer. *All!* As the well-known hymn proclaims, "Your sin, not in part but the whole, has been nailed to the cross and you bear it no more."[5] Now if God has forgiven us of everything, every iota, every unkind word, every jealous thought, what right do we have to hold something over another person?

This same loving and merciful God commands us to forgive others. He doesn't say if we have been unfairly wronged, then we don't need to forgive. He doesn't tell us that we only need to forgive if the other person says she is sorry. Even if the offender doesn't realize the offense, God doesn't let us out of the obligation to forgive. No, we are to follow Jesus' own example of forgiving those who nailed Him to the cross.

To me, this chapter is one of the most important in this book, because it concerns an essential principle in the Christian life, not only for us moms but also for our family members. If we truly grasp the gospel message—that

God is incredibly serious about forgiveness. Are you?

through Christ our sins are forgiven—then the natural outpouring of this truth is for us to offer forgiveness to others. Again, I'm not saying that we should let others walk over us like doormats, but rather that we should forgive and set boundaries with others if necessary. Forgiving is a positive step in the direction of hope.

What did Jesus mean when He said, "For if you forgive men their trespasses, your heavenly Father will also forgive you. But if you do not forgive men their trespasses, neither will your Father forgive your trespasses" (Matt. 6:14–15 NKJV)? That's a hard passage, and frankly I've ignored it for years. It comes down to this: if we don't forgive someone, then we are not grasping the gospel message. God is incredibly serious about forgiveness. Are you?

Love Notes from God

Out of the depths I have cried to You, O LORD;
Lord, hear my voice!
Let Your ears be attentive
To the voice of my supplications.

If You, LORD, should mark iniquities,
O Lord, who could stand?
But there is forgiveness with You,
That You may be feared.

I wait for the LORD, my soul waits,
And in His word I do hope.
My soul waits for the Lord
More than those who watch for the morning—
Yes, more than those who watch for the morning.

O Israel, hope in the LORD;
For with the LORD there is mercy,
And with Him is abundant redemption.
And He shall redeem Israel
From all his iniquities. (Ps. 130 NKJV)

In the New Living Translation, the last verses of Psalm 130 read, "O Israel, hope in the LORD; for with the LORD there is unfailing love and an overflowing supply of salvation. He himself will free Israel from every kind of sin." Oh, how beautiful is God's unfailing love! It has an overflowing supply of forgiveness. God's love is superabundant and filled with grace.

I find myself crying out to God asking for even an ounce of His beautiful love to offer to the people around me. His merciful love frees us. May our Christlike love free others.

▪ ▪ ▪

In what ways do my kids see the beauty of forgiveness through my own example as I relate to others?

Inspiring a Love Relationship
With God

You shall love the LORD your God with all your heart,
with all your soul, and with all your strength.
—DEUTERONOMY 6:5 NKJV

When I love God more than I love my earthly dearest,
then I shall love my earthly dearest more than I do now.
—C. S. LEWIS

What is the most important life lesson we can teach our kids? Perhaps after reading the last chapter, you are thinking forgiveness. Maybe you are thinking kindness or compassion toward others. One could also argue that obedience and respect are paramount to becoming a wise and mature adult. Yes, all of these are important qualities we must teach our kids as they grow and mature. But what is the one thing we don't want to miss? The lesson above all lessons?

God told the Israelites the most important message to teach their kids—and thousands of years later, it's still the most important lesson.

No, I'm not referring to the Ten Commandments although we do want to teach those to our kids. I'm referring the Great Commandment. "Hear, O Israel: The LORD our God, the LORD is one! You shall love the LORD your God with all your heart, with all your soul, and with all your strength" (Deut. 6:4–5 NKJV). Jesus reiterated this in the New Testament when a lawyer asked Him which was the greatest commandment. Jesus answered, "The first of all the commandments is 'Hear, O Israel, the LORD our God, the LORD is one. And you shall love the LORD your God with all your heart, with all your soul, with all your mind, and with all your strength.' This is the first commandment. And the second, like it, is this: 'You shall love your neighbor as yourself.' There is no other commandment greater than these" (Mark 12:29–31 NKJV).

Isn't it interesting that in a culture where we parents are so busy making sure our kids are on the best soccer teams or in the best schools and learn gymnastics at age three or start art lessons at five, we often overlook the most important lesson of all? God told the Israelite parents it was their job to teach their children to love God. Interestingly, He begins by implying this great truth must be a part of their own lives. God said, "And these words which I command you today shall be in your heart. You shall teach them diligently to your children, and shall talk of them when you sit in your house, when you walk by the way, when you lie down, and when you rise up" (Deut. 6:6–7 NKJV).

Practical Ways to Build a Love for God

God is serious about parents teaching their kids to love Him. The passage says we must teach them diligently, so we must be intentional about teaching our kids to love God. It shouldn't be a haphazard whim, nor should this instruction be solely left up to the church or Christian school. First and foremost, it is our role as parents. We must look for those teachable moments at the dinner table, when we are going to the store, while we are sitting down to read, or when we tuck our children in bed at night.

How do we build a love for God in our family? The answer is actually quite simple: by teaching our kids who God is. What are His attributes? What does God say about Himself? We find the answers in the Bible. You can begin reading Bible stories to your kids at an early age. There are many children's Bibles available at Christian bookstores or online retailers. Some of my favorites include the *Beginners Bible*, *My First Study Bible*, and the *Day by Day Kids Bible*.[1]

> When we recognize who God is and His love for us, we can't help but love Him in return.

As your kids grow older, encourage them to begin reading the Bible on their own. Ask them to accompany you to the bookstore, and include them in the process of selecting their own Bibles. There are many teen Bibles on the market today. Talk to your kids about what you are learning about God in your own Bible reading. Allow your kids to see you reading God's Word and know your love for His Word. Discuss the Bible and God's attributes at the dinner table and share tidbits with them throughout the day. One of my favorite devotionals to do with the family at the dinner table is *Sticky Situations* by Betsy Schmitt.[2]

When we recognize who God is and His love for us, we can't help but love Him in return. He is the sovereign and holy God, Creator of all things. He is merciful, gracious, and kind. He is the Good Shepherd who tenderly cares for His sheep. I am continually amazed to think that the King of kings and Lord of lords hears my prayers and cares about me. The Bible teaches me how wonderful He is. When we saturate ourselves with the truth about God's goodness and love, it can't help but overflow from our actions and words and pour into our children's lives.

Praying Kids

One of the greatest concepts we can pass down to our kids to help them in their own personal spiritual walk is a passion for prayer—praying always as they lay their burdens at God's feet. We want our children to know they have the greatest opportunity on earth: the opportunity to converse with the Creator of the universe and the Lover of their souls. The sovereign God, the high King of heaven invites us to cast our burdens on Him. When we pray, we turn our hearts and minds toward Him and away from our frustrations, annoyances, and difficulties.

Prayer transforms us from weak and worried people to faith-filled, God-confident warriors. Let us be faithful to teach our kids the joy of conversing with God in prayer. First, our kids need to see our own personal love and devotion to prayer. Tell your kids you are praying for them. Keep a prayer journal to show them how God has answered your prayers. Teach your family that prayer is not a magic wand that gives us everything we want. It is rather an opportunity for us to lay everything at God's feet and trust His wisdom.

> Prayer transforms us from weak and worried people to faith-filled, God-confident warriors.

Let's teach our kids that prayer is more than just asking for stuff. Prayer involves praising God for who He is, confessing our sin and need for Him, thanking God for His blessings, and seeking His help.

We can teach our children these elements of prayer as we pray together at meals, before going to bed, and throughout the day. As our kids enter their elementary years, we can encourage them to pray on their own as they wake up each morning. Don't be dogmatic or forceful when it comes to spiritual things. God wants our hearts, not a forced ritual. Our kids grow to love prayer as they experience the joy and blessing and fruit of drawing close to God themselves. Oh, what contentment we can find as we walk day by day in fellowship with our heavenly Father!

So You're Not Perfect

So you've made a few mistakes along the way. You have a few regrets. Join the club. We wish we could be brightly shining beacons of God's love in our homes, yet we may feel like weak flames that continually flicker out and need to be relit. Bottom line: we need God. We need His grace, strength, love, and power. We are in need of His wisdom and discernment when it comes to every area of parenting. As you read this book, and especially this chapter, don't wallow in regret of things not done or mistakes you have made. Instead, move forward by teaching your kids to love the Lord and love each other.

You can begin today to move in a positive direction. The place to begin is with your own relationship with the Lord. Walk with Him. Draw close to Him. Get to know His abundant love for you. Seek Him to help you parent each day and move away from anger and toward love. If necessary, humbly apologize to any family members whom you have hurt with your words or actions, and then move forward in a direction of loving your family and making a difference in their lives.

Jesus said, "Blessed are the poor in spirit, for theirs is the kingdom of heaven" (Matt. 5:3). In this verse, the phrase "the poor in spirit" literally means those who recognize their utter and desperate need for God. In other words, Jesus is saying, "Happy and fortunate are those of you who know how much you need God." The opposite of those who are poor in spirit are those who rely on their own self-sufficiency and self-righteousness in an effort to live the Christian life in their own power and strength. Yet Jesus calls us to abide in Him, for without Him we can do nothing (John 15:5).

My dear friend, you are not alone in your role of motherhood. You have a loving God who is willing to walk beside you and give you strength and wisdom each day. Each day is a new day. Move forward, trusting Him day by day. He is your keeper, your loving provider, your sufficiency, and your friend. Look to Him, for "those who look to him are radiant; their faces are never covered with shame" (Ps. 34:5).

Love Notes from God

Through the LORD's mercies we are not consumed,
Because His compassions fail not.
They are new every morning;
Great is Your faithfulness.
"The LORD is my portion," says my soul,
"Therefore I hope in Him!"

The LORD is good to those who wait for Him,
To the soul who seeks Him.
It is good that one should hope and wait quietly
For the salvation of the LORD. (Lam. 3:22–26 NKJV)

Aren't you thankful for a loving God who desires us to put our hope in Him? He wants us to come to Him and bring Him our broken hearts and messed-up lives, for He is faithful. He is able to sustain us. He is able to give us what we need to parent with love and wisdom. He never leaves us.

How comforting it is to know that His compassion is new every morning! Yesterday is done, so let us press forward in His strength as we begin each day in the confidence of His love.

■ ■ ■

Am I seeking God for my hope and help as I raise my children, or am I trying to parent on my own?

How will I actively seek God each day?

Notes

Chapter 3: Seven Healthy Ways to Handle Anger
1. James Bone, "Cheated Bride Who Said 'I Don't' Turns Her Wedding Day into a Charity Event," www.timesonline.co.uk/article/ 0,11069-2349509.html.
2. The Better Health Channel, www.betterhealth.vic.gov.au. The Better Health Channel is part of the Department of Human Services, Victoria, Australia.
3. For more information on these organizations, go to www.mops.org, www.hearts-at-home.org, or do an online search for "early childhood PTA" in your city.

Chapter 4: The Hidden B's in Our Bonnets
1. Martha Beck, "Yes, It Was Awful—Now Please Shut Up," *O* magazine, July 2006, 46.
2. Frederick Buechner, *Telling Secrets* (San Francisco: HarperSanFrancisco, 1992), 33.

Chapter 7: What to Do with a Crying Baby
1. Maud Meates-Dennis, "What to Do with a Crying Baby—Will Picking ?Her Up Spoil Her?", EzineArticles.com, http://ezinearticles.com/ What-to-do-With-a-Crying-Baby—Will-Picking-Her-Up-Spoil-Her?&id=291561.
2. http://www.mayoclinic.com/healthy/healthy-baby/PR00037.
3. For more information on the Miracle Blanket, go to www.miracleblanket.com.
4. http://www.mayoclinic.com/healthy/healthy-baby/PR00037.
5. For more information, visit www.WomensHealth.gov or call 1-800-994-9662.

Chapter 8: Stopping the Mommy Explosion
1. Adapted from Lowell D. Streiker, ed., *Nelson's Big Book of Laughter* (Nashville: Thomas Nelson, 2000), 302–3.

Chapter 9: Understanding Your Child
1. Ross Campbell, MD, *How to Really Parent Your Child* (Nashville: W Publishing Group, 2005), 95.

Chapter 10: Riding the Storms of Adolescent Hormones

1. Barbara P. Homeier, MD, "A Parent's Guide to Surviving the Teen Years," http://kidshealth.org/parent/growth/growing/adolescence.html.

2. James Dobson, *Complete Marriage and Family Home Reference Guide* (Wheaton, IL: Tyndale, 2000), 213.

3. Barbara Wood, "Understanding adolescence: Respect is Key, says author in talk here," The Almanac, March 20, 2002, www.almanacnews.com/morgue/2002/2002-03_20.stepp1.html.

4. Story by James Dobson found in Mike Yorkey, ed., *Growing a Healthy Family* (Brentwood, TN: Wolgemuth & Hyatt, 1990), 196–97.

5. Ross Campbell, MD, *How to Really Parent Your Teenager* (Nashville: W Publishing Group, 2006), 22.

6. Paul David Tripp, *Age of Opportunity* (Phillipsburg, NJ: Presbyterian and Reformed Publishing, 1997), 17.

7. Tim Kimmel, *Why Christian Kids Rebel* (Nashville: W Publishing Group, 2004), 10.

Chapter 11: How to Respond to Your Spouse's Anger

1. Stephen Arterburn and David Stoop, *Boiling Point* (Nashville: W Publishing Group, 1991), 5.

2. Ibid., 26, 114.

3. Dr. Henry Cloud and Dr. John Townsend, *Boundaries* (Grand Rapids: Zondervan, 1992), 157.

4. Ibid.

5. If you or someone you know is affected by a loved one's alcoholism, find an Alcoholics Anonymous or Alateen meeting near you at www.al-anon.alateen.org.

6. http://www.springtideresources.org/resources/show.cfm?id=34.

Chapter 12: Portrait of a Loving Family

1. Tedd Tripp, *Shepherding a Child's Heart* (Wapwallopen, PA: Shepherd Press, 1995); Campbell, *How to Really Parent Your Child*; Tim Kimmel, *Grace-Based Parenting* (Nashville: W Publishing Group, 2004).

2. Martin Walsh, quoted in *How to Be an Up Person in a Down World* (Tulsa, OK: Honor, 1994), 107.

Chapter 13: Teaching Your Kids Genuine Compassion

1. Henry Van Dyke, quoted in *How to Be an Up Person in a Down World* (Tulsa, OK: Honor, 1994), 138.

Chapter 14: Happiness Is a Family Full of Forgiveness

1. Ray Pritchard, *The Healing Power of Forgiveness* (Eugene, OR: Harvest House, 2005), 11.

2. If you want to talk with someone about what it means to place your faith in Christ, please call 1-888-NEED-HIM.

3. Pritchard, *The Healing Power of Forgiveness*, 77.

4. James Dobson, *Love Must Be Tough* (Nashville: W Publishing Group, 1996); Cloud and Townsend, *Boundaries.*

5. "It Is Well with My Soul," lyrics by Horatio G. Spafford (1828–1888), public domain.

Chapter 15: Inspiring a Love Relationship with God

1. *Beginners Bible* (Grand Rapids: Zonderkidz, 1997), *My First Study Bible* (Nashville: Tommy Nelson, 1994), and the *Day by Day Kids Bible* (Wheaton, IL: Tyndale Kids, 2002).

2. Betsy Schmitt, *Sticky Situations* (Wheaton, IL: Tyndale Kids, 2006).

About the Author

Karol Ladd offers lasting hope and biblical truth to women around the world through her uplifting books. A former teacher and gifted communicator, Karol is a popular speaker to women's organizations, church groups, and corporate events. She is a frequent guest on radio and television programs and is the best-selling author of more than twenty books. Her most valued role is that of wife to Curt and mother to daughters Grace and Joy.

Visit Karol's Web site at PositiveMom.com.

Also available from KAROL LADD

ISBN: 0-8499-0711-X

ISBN: 0-8499-0616-4

ISBN: 1-4041-0428-3

ISBN: 1-4041-0449-6